JOHNNY
TREMAIN

Esther Forbes

TECHNICAL DIRECTOR Maxwell Krohn
EDITORIAL DIRECTOR Justin Kestler
MANAGING EDITOR Ben Florman

SERIES EDITORS Boomie Aglietti, Justin Kestler
PRODUCTION Christian Lorentzen

WRITERS Selena Ward, Yael Goldstein
EDITORS Karen Schrier, John Crowther

This edition published by Spark Publishing

Spark Publishing
A Division of SparkNotes LLC
120 Fifth Avenue, 8th Floor
New York, NY 10011

02 03 04 05 SN 9 8 7 6 5 4 3 2 1

Please send all comments and questions or report errors to
feedback@sparknotes.com.

Library of Congress information available upon request

Printed and bound in the United States

RRD-C

ISBN 1-58663-523-9

INTRODUCTION: STOPPING TO BUY SPARKNOTES ON A SNOWY EVENING

Whose words these are you *think* you know.
Your paper's due tomorrow, though;
We're glad to see you stopping here
To get some help before you go.

Lost your course? You'll find it here.
Face tests and essays without fear.
Between the words, good grades at stake:
Get great results throughout the year.

Once school bells caused your heart to quake
As teachers circled each mistake.
Use SparkNotes and no longer weep,
Ace every single test you take.

Yes, books are lovely, dark, and deep,
But only what you grasp you keep,
With hours to go before you sleep,
With hours to go before you sleep.

CONTENTS

NOTE: This SparkNote refers to the Yearling Newbery edition of *Johnny Tremain*, published by Bantam Doubleday Dell. The novel was originally published in 1943.

CONTEXT

ESTHER FORBES was born on June 28, 1891, in rural Massachusetts to a family steeped in American history. Her mother, Harriet Forbes, was an antiquarian specializing in the New England area, and the Forbes home was filled with relics of the region's past. The Forbes family also eagerly traded folklore, particularly a story about an ancestor who was accused of witchcraft. From a very young age, Forbes began to read widely, paying particular attention to books on history and stories set within a historical context.

After graduating from high school at the Bradford Academy, Forbes spent two years studying history at the University of Wisconsin. When the United States entered World War I, she left college to join the war effort. Just like Johnny Tremain, war transformed her life and her ambitions. Forbes spent several years working on a Virginia farm to produce food for the embattled nation, which she calls the proudest years of her life. After the war ended, she moved back to Massachusetts and worked as an editor at the Boston-based publishing company Houghton Mifflin. During this period she also devoted a lot of time to her own writing. She published her first novel, *O Genteel Lady!*, in 1926, and published four more historical novels over the course of the next decade. In 1942 she published her first nonfiction work, a biography of Paul Revere entitled *Paul Revere and the World He Lived In*, for which she won the Pulitzer Prize.

While researching Paul Revere's life, Forbes became increasingly interested in the colonial period, particularly in the Bostonians of the Revolutionary era. She decided to write a children's book telling the story of a young Boston apprentice who witnesses America's birth firsthand. Forbes began writing *Johnny Tremain* on December 8, 1941, the day after Pearl Harbor was bombed and the United States entered World War II. As the war waged on, Forbes was impressed with the way that young men and women were suddenly forced to become adults and take on weighty responsibilities. She admired their sense of self-sacrifice and their commitment to the cause of patriotism. Her observations of American youth during World War II helped her to understand the youth of the Revolutionary era and the ways in which they, too, were forced to grow up rapidly. These observations helped Forbes to develop the characters of Johnny and Rab.

Johnny Tremain was published to widespread acclaim in 1943, during the height of American engagement in World War II. In 1944 *Johnny Tremain* received the Newbery Medal, awarded annually to the best book of children's literature. After *Johnny Tremain*, Forbes returned to publishing novels for adults. Forbes's best-selling book *The Running of the Tide* won the MGM novel award and inspired a motion picture. Her last work, *Rainbow on the Road*, spawned the 1969 musical *Come Summer*. Forbes died on August 12, 1967, after a long and fruitful career as a novelist, historian, and biographer.

Though *Johnny Tremain* is one of only two books Forbes wrote for children, it is the work for which she is best known today. The novel has become standard reading for students because of its insightful and vivid portrayal of the events leading up to the Revolutionary War. During the time period that the book covers, colonial frustrations are reaching a fever pitch and threatening to erupt into war. In the wake of the French and Indian War, also known as the Seven Years War, England found itself heavily in debt and looked to the colonists to alleviate some of the financial pressure. Between 1764 and 1767, the British government enacted a series of new taxes targeting to the colonies, such as the Sugar Tax, the Townshend Acts, and the notorious Stamp Tax. Given that the war had been fought partly to protect the American colonists, the decision to raise revenue from within the colonies made some sense, but it outraged many Americans, who felt that they were being governed unfairly. Since Americans had no representative in Parliament, they argued that they had no say in how they were taxed or how their tax money was spent. The Americans called England's unfair financial practice "taxation without representation."

The Americans responded to England's actions by ignoring the laws, formally protesting the British violation of American rights, and finally by resorting to boycotts and outright violence. England repealed many of the taxes in response to American protest, and the years 1770 to 1773 saw a lull in the difficulties between the mother country and her colonies, although the rebel leaders continued to criticize England. In 1773, the year in which *Johnny Tremain* begins, this lull in civil unrest was broken. The disruptive incident was the infamous Boston Tea Party, during which young patriots, dressed as Native Americans, stormed a British ship and tossed its cargo of tea into Boston Harbor. This act of disobedience, and the British response, set off a series of events that led to the Revolutionary War. *Johnny Tremain* brings to life this series of events, and the lives of the men and women involved in them.

PLOT OVERVIEW

OURTEEN-YEAR-OLD Johnny Tremain is the gifted apprentice of Ephraim Lapham, a silversmith in Revolutionary-era Boston. The pious and elderly Mr. Lapham is more interested in preparing his own soul for death than in running his silver shop, so Johnny is the chief breadwinner of the family. Dove and Dusty, Lapham's other apprentices, are expected to bow to Johnny's authority, and Mrs. Lapham is determined to have Johnny marry her daughter Cilla. Johnny's enormous talent and his special status in the Lapham household go to his head, and Johnny often bullies the lazy, insolent Dove, as well as Dusty and the four Lapham daughters. Although Mr. Lapham tries to contain Johnny's arrogance, Johnny is unwilling to rein in his quick temper or impulsive acts.

The Lapham's fortune and Johnny's fame as a silversmith appear to take a turn for the better when the wealthy merchant John Hancock puts in an order for an elaborate silver basin. Mr. Lapham hesitates to take on such a difficult project, but the rash Johnny accepts the job on behalf of his master. That night, Johnny reveals his family secret to Cilla. He is related to Jonathan Lyte, a wealthy Boston merchant. Johnny's mother revealed his ancestry to him before she died, and she gave him a silver cup engraved with the Lyte family's coat of arms. She instructed him to steer clear of the Lytes unless he had no other recourse.

Johnny struggles to design the silver basin's handles, but he is dissatisfied with the result. After consulting Paul Revere, Johnny creates a mold for a perfect set of handles. While he is casting the wax model in silver, Dove deliberately hands him a cracked crucible. Dove's intention is only to humble Johnny by playing a practical joke on him, but his prank results in a terrible accident that disfigures Johnny's hand. No longer able to work as a silversmith's apprentice, Johnny loses his status in the Lapham household. After the burn heals, Mrs. Lapham begins to complain of Johnny's idleness and the expense of feeding him. She begins negotiating a business partnership with Mr. Tweedie, a silversmith from Baltimore, and forbids Johnny from marrying Cilla. Mr. Lapham urges Johnny to find a new trade, but promises to house him until he finds a new master. During his fruitless search, Johnny drops into Mr. Lorne's print shop, where a Whig newspaper, the *Boston Observer*, is published. Mr. Lorne's enigmatic nephew and apprentice Rab immediately intrigues Johnny. Johnny confides the story of his accident to Rab, and the boy promises Johnny a job delivering newspapers if he fails to find any skilled labor.

Depressed and desperately trying to find a new craft, Johnny finally decides to approach Jonathan Lyte. He produces his silver cup as proof of their kinship, but Lyte accuses Johnny of stealing the valuable heirloom and has the boy arrested. Johnny appeals to Rab for assistance, and Rab not only finds a lawyer to defend him for free but also arranges to have Cilla testify in his favor. After Johnny is cleared of the charges, he tries to sell the cup to Lyte, but Lyte steals it from him. Only then does Johnny approach Lorne to ask for the delivery job.

While delivering newspapers, Johnny becomes well acquainted with the key members in Boston politics and is transformed from an apathetic political bystander into an ardent Whig. The Lornes treat him kindly, as if he were a member of their family. Johnny participates in the Boston Tea Party, and becomes a confidant, small-time Whig spy, and errand boy for all the Whigs of Boston. During this period of Whig scheming, in the months leading up the Revolutionary War, Johnny slowly changes from a selfish, arrogant child into a selfless, idealistic man. Rab's quiet influence teaches Johnny to control his temper, and the colonial situation provides Johnny with something larger than himself to care about. Johnny also matures through his growing recognition of his feelings for Cilla, who has gone to work as a servant in the Lyte home.

On the eve of war between the colonists and Britain, the Tory Lytes plan to flee to England. Immediately before their departure, Lavinia Lyte approaches Johnny to tell him that she has investigated his claims of kinship and found them to be legitimate. She insists that her father had sincerely believed that Johnny was lying when he accused him, but admits that both father and daughter recognize that Johnny has a right to some of the Lyte property.

Rab is mortally wounded when war breaks out in the battle of Lexington. Johnny is deeply shaken by Rab's death, but he vows to continue the struggle for the human rights for which Rab sacrificed his life. Doctor Warren, an esteemed rebel leader, examines Johnny's hand while Rab's lifeless body lies upstairs. He discovers that the thumb is fused to the palm by nothing but scar tissue, and that Johnny's handicap can be easily remedied with minor surgery. Although he cannot promise that Johnny will ever be a silversmith again, he assures Johnny that he will soon be able to fire the musket that Rab bequeathed to him before dying.

CHARACTER LIST

Jonathan Tremain The protagonist of the novel. Johnny is the fourteen-year-old prize apprentice of the Boston silversmith Ephraim Lapham. Johnny is a talented craftsman, but he is also arrogant, rash, and slightly cruel; he gains pleasure tormenting the two other apprentices, Dusty and Dove, by touting his superiority. When Johnny's hand is disfigured in an accident, he can no longer work as a silversmith, and his sense of self is imperiled. As the rebellious colonists begin to fight England for their identity, Johnny finds a new life among the leaders of the Boston Whig party and finds himself transformed from a selfish youth into a patriotic young man.

Rab Silsbee Johnny's best friend. With his quiet, unassuming confidence, Rab becomes Johnny's model and guide as Johnny struggles to find a new identity. Rab introduces Johnny to the world of revolutionary politics.

Priscilla Lapham The third oldest daughter of Mrs. Lapham. Cilla is loyal, selfless, and caring. Although her primary devotion is to her younger sister, Isannah, Cilla's feelings for Johnny help him to develop into a warm, patient, honest young man.

Ephraim Lapham A Boston silversmith. Mr. Lapham is a pious and kind man who acts as Johnny's master before the accident that disfigures his hand. Mr. Lapham attempts to teach Johnny humility by referring to the Bible and reminding him of the dangers of pride and arrogance, but Johnny pays little attention to these warnings.

Lavinia Lyte Tremain Johnny's mother. Lavinia Tremain defied her wealthy family's wishes when she married Charles Tremain, a French prisoner of war being held in Boston. When her husband died, she raised Johnny on her own by sewing to make money. She revealed her wealthy origins to her son only on her deathbed.

Charles Tremain Johnny's father. Charles Tremain, known in Boston as Charles Latour, was a French soldier taken as a British prisoner during the French and Indian War. While he was held as a prisoner in Boston, he met and wooed Johnny's mother. After they married, Johnny's parents traveled to France, where Charles died of cholera.

Isannah Lapham The youngest daughter of Mrs. Lapham. Isannah is selfish and vain, and beloved by Cilla. Isannah's golden-haired, ethereal beauty attracts a great deal of attention, most significantly from Lavinia Lyte. Lavinia takes Isannah into her care and introduces her to high society, separating her from her family and their lower-class ways of life.

Dove An apprentice at the Lapham house. Dove is lazy, dishonest, and stupid. He is responsible for Johnny's hand injury.

Lavinia Lyte Jonathan Lyte's beautiful, arrogant, and regal daughter. Enchanted by Isannah's ethereal beauty, Lavinia Lyte takes the child away from her family, and slowly weakens the bond between Isannah and her sister Cilla.

Jonathan Lyte A wealthy Boston merchant and Johnny's great-uncle. Crooked and cruel, Lyte tries to make a profit by making friends on both sides of the colonial struggle, but as tensions mount in Boston, Lyte is exposed as a Tory. On the eve of war, Lyte and his family depart for London.

Mrs. Lapham Ephraim Lapham's daughter-in-law. Mrs. Lapham is a dedicated, hardworking mother and a no-nonsense taskmaster to the apprentices. She works as the housekeeper in Mr. Lapham's house.

Dorcas Lapham Mrs. Lapham's second daughter. Although Dorcas longs to be elegant and sophisticated, she ends up falling in love with the poverty-stricken Frizel, Jr., and elopes to avoid having to marry Mr. Tweedie.

Madge Lapham Mrs. Lapham's oldest daughter. Like Mrs. Lapham, Madge is tough and capable. She elopes with Sergeant Gale, a British soldier.

Dusty Mr. Lapham's youngest apprentice. Dusty runs away to sea after Johnny leaves Mr. Lapham's silver shop.

Mr. Lorne Rab's uncle and master. Mr. Lorne owns the print shop that publishes the *Boston Observer*, a rebellious Whig newspaper.

Mrs. Lorne Mr. Lorne's wife. Mrs. Lorne sees through Johnny's scornful and arrogant exterior to the lonely boy inside. She treats him like a son and becomes like a second mother to him.

Mr. Tweedie A silversmith who becomes Mr. Lapham's business partner after Johnny's accident. When none of her daughters will marry him, Mrs. Lapham marries Tweedie to ensure that the silver shop stays in the Lapham family.

Samuel Adams A leader of the Revolutionary forces in Boston. Samuel Adams was considered the greatest creator of propaganda for the rebel cause. He wrote numerous pamphlets inciting and inspiring the revolution.

John Hancock One of the wealthiest men in Boston and a leader of the Revolutionary forces. Johnny disfigures his hand while making a silver basin for him.

Doctor Warren One of the leaders of the Revolutionary forces in Boston. He fixes Johnny's disfigured hand at the end of the novel.

Paul Revere A master silversmith and one of the leaders of the Revolutionary forces in Boston.

Governor Hutchinson The governor of Massachusetts. Governor Hutchinson refuses to send the tea ships back to London, which incites the Boston Tea Party. After the tea incident, he is called back to England.

James Otis The founder of the Boston Observers, a secret rebel organization that meets in Mr. Lorne's print shop. James Otis's fellow club members acknowledge his intellectual brilliance, but his mental instability frightens and endangers them.

Josiah Quincy A prominent Whig lawyer. Quincy successfully defends Johnny against Lyte's charge of theft.

Colonel Smith A British officer stationed in Boston. Johnny keeps close tabs on his movements and reports back to the leaders of the Revolution.

Lieutenant Stranger A kind and friendly British officer stationed in Boston. He develops a strained friendship with Johnny.

Mrs. Bessie The Lytes' cook and Cilla's only friend in the Lyte household. Mrs. Bessie is an ardent Whig and a confidante of Samuel Adams, but she nonetheless remains loyal to her Tory employers.

Lydia The black washerwoman at the Afric Queen, a tavern where many British officers sleep. Lydia is a rebel sympathizer who, because of her connection to the British soldiers, gathers information for the rebel forces.

Pumpkin A British soldier stationed in Boston. Pumpkin wants to abandon his duties and buy a farm. Because he is poor, he can only achieve his dream in America. Johnny helps him desert from the army, but Pumpkin is captured and executed.

Sewall A poor relative of the Lytes who works as a clerk in Jonathan Lyte's office. Sewall is kind and brave; he runs off to join the Minute Men.

Sergeant Gale A British officer who marries Madge Lapham.

General Gage The British general placed in charge of the Boston troops once Governor Hutchinson is recalled to London.

ANALYSIS OF MAJOR CHARACTERS

JOHNNY TREMAIN

The title character and hero of *Johnny Tremain* is a fourteen-year old boy living in colonial Boston. When we first meet Johnny, he is arrogant, ambitious, slightly cruel, and wholly self-centered. In part, these vicious character traits stem from his prodigious gifts: he is unusually bright and well educated for an apprentice, and he is widely considered the most talented young silversmith in Boston. His insecurity and cruelty may also stem from his lack of a loving family, as his parents died when he was very young. Johnny works as an apprentice in a silversmith's house, learning the craft in the hope that one day he can open his own shop. As an apprentice in his master's house, Johnny has a status only a little above a servant, but he acts as tyrant, ordering around not only the other two apprentices but even his master and his master's four granddaughters.

Johnny's disdainful treatment of others leads to resentment, and this resentment leads to a disfiguring accident that ruins Johnny's future as a silversmith. With a crippled hand, Johnny cannot find skilled work, and he allows himself to feel self-pity and despair. Dangerously close to giving up all hope of an honest life, Johnny almost turns to crime. Yet, due to his new job with the *Boston Observer*, the Whig newspaper, and his friendship with Rab Silsbee, the Lornes, and the leaders of the revolution, Johnny takes a more honest path. Inspired by their idealism and self-sacrifice, Johnny finds himself transforming from a selfish boy into a patriotic man. On a conscious level, he models himself after his new best friend, Rab, trying to imitate the older boy's quiet, unassuming confidence and mild temperament. Unconsciously, as Johnny devours books in the Lornes' library and soaks in the rhetoric of such acquaintances as Samuel Adams and James Otis, he begins to care about something much larger than his own petty ambitions and comforts. Johnny suddenly becomes an ardent Whig and a soldier, not because he is part of the Lorne family but because he rationally believes in freedom and rights for the colonists. At the novel's end, Johnny has finally overcome his psychological and emotional handicaps. Faced unexpectedly with the prospect of a restored hand, Johnny is less concerned about whether he will be able to resume his job as a silversmith than whether he will be able to fire a gun and serve his nascent country.

RAB SILSBEE

Rab is two years older than Johnny, and when they first meet, he is everything that Johnny is not. Rab's quiet confidence and sense of self makes him a foil for Johnny, who is still uncertain of his role in the world. Rab is quiet where Johnny is talkative, unassuming where Johnny is proud, and patient where Johnny is impetuous. From their very first meeting, Johnny sees Rab as a model and the man that he wants to become. Nonjudgmental and open-minded, Rab is immediately able to see through Johnny's brash exterior to his sincere and lonely inner self. Rab reaches out to him effectively, providing him with a new life. He does not pity Johnny for his crippled hand and lost job. Instead, he offers Johnny the opportunity to overcome his handicaps.

Although Rab is only sixteen years old, he seems to feel comfortable in the world of high politics. He is trusted by all of the most important Revolutionary War leaders, who rely on him to print the Whig paper called the *Boston Observer*. Rab appears introverted and unflappable, but he harbors strong passions just below the surface. A devoted patriot and ideologue, Rab is a born fighter. He is fearless and thrives during times of strife because he is passionate and believes deeply in human rights. As soon as militias begin to form to fight against the British government, Rab joins the Minute Men. Forbes suggests that just as Rab makes an ardent fighter, he could also make an ardent lover. One of the only two times that Johnny sees Rab animated is during a party at which Rab dances with every girl present, and Rab's secret courtship of Cilla hints at deep, passionate feelings. Rab is never given the chance to explore his second passion, though, as he is killed fulfilling his first. He is fatally shot at Lexington, during the opening battle of the Revolutionary War.

CILLA LAPHAM

Cilla is the granddaughter of Johnny's master, the silversmith Ephraim Lapham. At the book's start, fourteen-year-old Cilla is promised to Johnny in marriage because of an economic arrangement to keep the silver shop in the Lapham family. Following Johnny's disfigurement, however, this arrangement is cancelled. Like Rab, Cilla seems to be Johnny's opposite in many ways. Though she is very bright, she is too self-effacing to demand to be taught how to read and write. Instead, she devotes her energy to her sickly, but beautiful, younger sister, Isannah, using any extra money she can find to buy the spoiled child ribbons and other treats. Sensitive and thoughtful, Cilla secretly sneaks food into the impoverished Johnny's pockets in the interim period between his accident and his new home with Rab. When wealthy Lavinia Lyte becomes enchanted with Isannah, Cilla follows her sister to the Lyte home because she wants to accompany Isannah. Cilla works at the Lyte home as a lower-class servant, while Lavinia parades Isannah around Boston high society. As Lavinia cleverly tears Isannah away from Cilla, Cilla suffers silently and stoically.

On the other hand, Cilla has a caustic wit, teasing Johnny mercilessly and trading jabs with Rab. Cilla is self-reliant, a hard worker, and a kind person. Over the course of the book, Cilla develops from a skinny child into a beautiful young woman, and she begins to attract attention from men for the first time. Rab takes an interest in her, as does a young British soldier named Pumpkin, but it is Johnny that she has cared for all along. Like many colonists, she becomes an ardent Whig, and she refuses to leave for London with the rest of the Lyte household, including Isannah, on the eve of the Revolution. At the book's end, Cilla loses her sister but gains the boy she has always loved.

Themes, Motifs & Symbols

Themes

Themes are the fundamental and often universal ideas explored in a literary work.

War's Transformation of Boys into Men

When *Johnny Tremain* begins, the protagonist is a fourteen-year-old boy. The novel ends less than two years later, and Johnny Tremain is a sixteen-year-old man. His rapid maturation is largely a function of the extreme political climate of his time. As a messenger and spy for the colonial rebel leaders, Johnny is thrust into life-and-death circumstances. To protect himself and those he works for, he must abandon many of the childish proclivities of his past. Working as a small-time spy, he is forced to develop into a trustworthy, patient young man, since he might have to listen carefully to hours of conversation just to glean a small tidbit of information. He must also learn to restrain his quick temper and impetuousness to survive during the turbulent and dangerous Revolutionary period. Most dramatically, Johnny is forced to focus on something larger than his own individual concerns. Because of the war, Johnny must fight and die for the independence of his fellow colonists, and he turns his fervor and passions outward. He leaves behind his callow selfishness and becomes a steadfast, patriotic man, eager to fight and die for his country.

The preternatural maturity demanded of boys in times of war is also clearly exhibited in the character of Rab. When Johnny first encounters Rab, the sixteen-year-old boy is already a man: he is self-possessed, fearless, and ready to die for his beliefs. Rab seems almost unbelievably precocious. His advanced development becomes conceivable only when we realize that he has been involved in the secretive revolutionary effort for years already. Like Johnny and many other children of wartime, Rab is unable to indulge in the vices and luxuries of childhood.

Forbes wrote *Johnny Tremain* during World War II, just after Pearl Harbor was attacked. She noticed how young men are forced to grow up quickly in times of war, as they are suddenly responsible for the fate of their country and their fellow men, not just for their own goals and ambitions. Forbes fashioned the youths of her Revolutionary War novel on her observations of the young soldiers fighting in World War II. Johnny Tremain, like the young men in World War II, could not control the circumstances in which fate placed him. Instead, he was forced to find his inner courage and become a self-assured adult.

THE REVOLUTION AS A COMING OF AGE

Johnny Tremain is a double coming-of-age story. It is not only the tale of Johnny's journey into adulthood, but also the story of the colonies' maturation into a nation. When we first meet Johnny, he chooses his battles very poorly. Rash and proud, he lashes out at anyone whom he thinks treats him with disrespect. Johnny, however, does not respect anyone else. He constantly torments his fellow apprentice Dove, and makes an enemy of a boy eager to be Johnny's friend. He becomes an enemy of the Baltimore silversmith Mr. Tweedie after he hurls an unprovoked barrage of outrageous insults at him. By extension, Johnny also angers Mrs. Lapham by placing her partnership with Tweedie in jeopardy. Finally, and most dangerously, Johnny unleashes his fury and outrage on Jonathan Lyte, one of the richest and most powerful men in Boston. Each of these thoughtless acts of anger eventually comes back to haunt Johnny. His poor relationship with Dove leads to his crippling accident, his provocation of Lyte leads to criminal prosecution, and the ill will that Mr. Tweedie and Mrs. Lapham bear him very nearly gets him hung on the gallows.

As Johnny befriends the Whigs of Boston, he undergoes many transformations. One of these transformations is a shedding of his truculent nature. Under Rab's tutelage, Johnny learns to control his outrage at petty offenses. Johnny does not suppress his fervor, as the pious pacifist Mr. Lapham would have preferred. Rather, Johnny redirects his passion into a worthy cause. Instead of petty and personal outrage, Johnny begins to feel a deep and meaningful commitment to a battle worth fighting for—a battle for freedom and for the equality of all men.

Johnny's cause is ultimately the colonies' cause, as the colonial rebels eventually choose to fight for the rights and freedom of men. Like Johnny, though, the colonists evolve from fighting petty skirmishes to a revolution for independence. After nearly a decade of boycotts and other minor insurrections, the rebel leaders finally conceive the compelling reasons for a war against Britain. Their ideology crystallizes, and the leaders make it clear that their cause is a fight for the equality of all mankind, rather than a small-minded fight for their own pocketbooks. With an understanding of their new ideology, and a grasp of the scale of their fight, they realize that boycotts and other minor rebellions are not the best means for their ends. The colonists realize that they must focus their efforts and fight a war for only one thing: independence. Once the colonists realize what is worth fighting for, they begin the process of maturing into a country.

THE INFLUENCE OF PERSONAL RELATIONSHIPS ON CHARACTER

Johnny's transformation from selfish child to selfless man begins when he meets Rab Silsbee. The immediate connection he feels to the understated, temperate Rab signals something deep within his own character that we did not see before. Johnny is drawn to the elements in Rab's character that are opposite to his own, and he soon finds himself trying to change to become more like Rab. Days after he first meets Rab, he is already comparing his own actions to Rab's and wondering what Rab would do in certain situations. The new Johnny that eventually emerges, we are led to believe, might never have existed had Johnny not chosen to build a friendship with Rab and Rab's world.

Johnny is not the only evolving character in the book. Isannah also has a choice of which path to take as she matures into a young woman. She might become gracious, noble, and passionate, or she might continue to build her selfish, arrogant, and conceited nature. As with Johnny, the path Isannah ultimately takes is determined by the choice she makes with regard to her friends. Instead of remaining loyal to her loving, kind sister, Isannah lets herself be seduced by the elegance and glamour of Lavinia Lyte. Under Lavinia's influence, Isannah's vices become even more pronounced. She becomes addicted to the fine clothes and food that Lavinia can provide, and she thrives on the doting attention she now receives from important people. When Isannah is asked to choose between Cilla and Lavinia forever, Isannah has already gone too far down a corrupted path to resist the high life that Lavinia offers her, and she leaves her sister behind.

THEMES

MOTIFS

Motifs are recurring structures, contrasts, or literary devices that can help to develop and inform the text's major themes.

PRIDE

In the opening chapter, Ephraim Lapham condemns the sin of pride, warning Johnny that "pride goeth before destruction, and an haughty spirit before a fall." Despite the negative way in which this motif is introduced, the novel does not portray pride as an entirely negative quality. Forbes reveals pride in many variations, and some version of the trait serves as a motivation for almost all of the main characters. The Lytes represent the worst sort of pride—a cruel, arrogant haughtiness that is often expressed as prejudice against the lower classes. They look down disapprovingly on all those of a lesser status, such as Johnny and Cilla. Rab, with his quiet self-possession and sense of purpose, shows the positive side of pride. Rab is proud of his work for the Whig rebellion, and, as a result, he works passionately to help the cause. Colonial rebel leaders such as Samuel Adams and John Hancock also exhibit a useful sort of pride. Their plucky cockiness enables them to declare war on a well-armed empire when they only have a few hundred untrained farmers to back up their threats.

Caught between the two possible paths of pride are two children, Isannah and Johnny, both of whom display tendencies toward excessive pride. Isannah's pride ultimately becomes haughty arrogance, because of her association with Lavinia Lyte. Johnny's pride, on the other hand, is recast under the guidance of Rab and the rebel leaders. His pride develops from an arrogant, defensive pride into a more effective, nobler sense of self. Johnny's final step away from his defensive pride occurs when he allows Doctor Warren to examine his crippled hand. Interestingly, Johnny's ultimate embrace of the loftier side of pride is indirectly a result of another prideful soul: his father. As a French prisoner of war in Boston, Charles Tremain was too proud to reveal his own name and spent a year responding to an assumed name, Charles Latour. The Bostonians knew this man as Latour, not Tremain. As a result, when Johnny turns up at Lyte's office claiming kinship, the name Tremain does not sound familiar to Mr. Lyte, and he is convinced that Johnny is an impostor. If Charles Tremain had not been too proud to keep his real name, Lyte may have taken Johnny in as his grandnephew. If Johnny had lived with the Lytes, however, he might have developed like Isannah, letting his pride develop into an arrogant haughtiness instead of a noble self-confidence and sense of purpose.

FORGIVENESS

When Johnny learns of Dove's malicious role in his crippling accident, Mr. Lapham admonishes him to forgive Dove, declaring, "I say, and Bible says, forgive." Mr. Lapham, as a pious Christian, seems to believe that every offense, no matter how horrific, should be forgiven. Mr. Lapham's beliefs not only make him gentle and mild in his personal relationships, but they also lead him to take a pacifist stance toward the conflict with England.

At the beginning of the book, Johnny's views on forgiveness could not be more opposite from those of Mr. Lapham. He refuses to forgive any offense, no matter how small. Even accidental offenses, such as when Samuel Adams's slave dumps water on Johnny's head, stir up Johnny's wrath. Mr. Lapham's limitless capacity for forgiveness seems very appealing, whereas Johnny's inability to forgive seems like a horrible flaw. Forbes, however, raises the issue of forgiveness within the context of revolution and thus challenges our moral judgment. Whereas Johnny does not forgive easily enough, we might ask whether Mr. Lapham forgives too easily. Forbes asks us to think about whether forgiveness is an appropriate response to the atrocious acts committed by the British.

Between the Whigs and the Tories, the Tories are more forgiving of British actions, and they are committed to being loyal to their mother country. As Forbes puts it, "Tories believ[ed] all differences could be settled with time, patience, and respect for government." The Whigs, on the other hand, do not want to resolve their issues with England and forgive the offenses they feel they have suffered; they want to fight. The book, however, suggests that the Whigs are the heroes, because they are fighting for human rights and independence. Even the mild-tempered Rab, who is held up as the model of perfect manhood, chooses on occasion to take revenge instead of pardoning others. When the butcher's son tortures the Webb twins, Rab does not forgive him, nor does he attempt a diplomatic resolution. Instead, he reacts with violence, physically hurting both the butcher and his son and damaging their shop. Forbes seems to suggest that, in some contexts, forgiving too easily might be just as bad as not forgiving easily enough.

CLASS

Compared to England, eighteenth-century America was a land of opportunity and equality. The colonies lacked both titled nobility and a poverty-stricken underclass. The vast majority of colonists were small farmers, and there were a handful of artisans, shopkeepers, unskilled laborers, and merchants in the cities. The minimal stratification that did exist was relatively fluid. With hard work and dedication, an ambitious farmer or servant could easily climb the ranks into the upper echelons of society. Forbes subtly interweaves this particular cultural difference between England and the colonies throughout the novel. We view the minimal social stratification of colonial society as represented in the wealthy Hancock's easy interaction with Ephraim Lapham, and even with a poor apprentice like Johnny. Johnny's interaction with Stranger illustrates the British side of this growing cultural divide. Stranger, a British officer, strictly observes the rules regarding class boundaries in his interactions with Johnny. Johnny, unused to such strict divisions among the classes, finds Stranger's behavior toward him inexplicable.

Forbes also portrays the social mobility that characterized life in the colonies. For example, the fact that an artisan like Paul Revere can become as influential and powerful as wealthy merchants like John Hancock and Samuel Adams—and can be treated as their equal—shows that class lines were easily crossed and often ignored in the colonies. The episode with Pumpkin further underscores the relative mobility of social class in the colonies as compared to in England. Pumpkin longs to desert the British army and become an American, because only in the colonies can a poor boy of low class hope to aspire above his birth station and acquire his own land. Forbes hints that the egalitarian nature of colonial life was one of the underlying causes of the growing dissatisfaction with British rule. Many democratically minded colonists, living in a society that was socially mobile rather than stratified, came to believe, as James Otis puts it in Chapter VIII, that "a handful of men cannot seize power over thousands. A man shall choose who it is shall rule over him."

SYMBOLS

Symbols are objects, characters, figures, or colors used to represent abstract ideas or concepts.

JOHNNY'S CRIPPLED HAND

Johnny's crippled hand is a physical symbol of the mental obstacle that cripples him, which is his arrogance and selfishness. Johnny develops the physical handicap as a direct result of his psychological handicap. Johnny's insufferable vanity and haughtiness drive Dove to resent Johnny. Dove plays a practical joke on Johnny to try to humble him and accidentally leaves Johnny with a disfigured hand. Unable to continue as a silversmith's apprentice, Johnny loses his sense of self and his ambitions for the future. Johnny is no longer the talented breadwinner for the Lapham family, and he must find other work.

Johnny's physical handicap forces him to think about his identity and grapple not only with his physical capabilities but also with his personality. As he struggles to come to terms with his new identity, he slowly overcomes his selfishness and arrogance. Johnny's self-pride turns into pride for his country, and his insolence turns into patience and kindness. Once Johnny fully overcomes his psychological handicap, he is able to mend his physical handicap as well. Johnny becomes secure enough with his own imperfections to allow Doctor Warren to examine and operate on his injured hand. Once the psychological handicap is gone, the physical handicap can also be overcome.

THE SILVER LYTE CUP

The silver cup, a luxury item bearing the seal of a powerful and wealthy family, is symbolic on two levels. First, the cup can be viewed as a symbol of Johnny's initial vices—his self-centered desires for money, status, and recognition. The cup is Johnny's only connection to the Lyte family. Presumably, the Lyte family is the genetic source for Johnny's vices, since they seem to exhibit these qualities in a much more drastic form than Johnny. When Lyte steals the cup from Johnny, he takes away Johnny's connection to the Lyte family and the vices that they represent. Cut off from his sole possession and his only relatives, Johnny is forced to adapt to his new situation and shed his selfish vices. When Johnny passes up the opportunity to take his cup back from Lyte, it signals that he no longer cares about his former selfish, materialistic ambitions.

The cup can also be viewed as a symbol of the world that fosters the vices that Johnny overcomes. In other words, it symbolizes Britain and the British mind-set with regard to class, money, and humanity. The connection works on a literal level, as the cup physically originated in England. Because the cup is a luxury item, it represents Britain's wealth, and the seal it bears symbolizes Britain's power and class-consciousness. By leaving behind the cup, then, Johnny renounces his selfish ambitions, but he also relinquishes his ties to England and the system of class and wealth that it nurtures. In letting go of the cup, he symbolically declares himself a citizen of America and not of England.

Johnny's Infatuation with Lavinia Lyte

Lavinia Lyte, with her haughtiness, wealth, and luxurious beauty, signifies, like the cup, the class-conscious world of England, where nobility of birth is more important than nobility of spirit. Lavinia prefers London to Boston and yearns to return there. She is embarrassed that her father works for a living, and would prefer that he become more like the titled nobility of England. In fact, at the book's end, as she and her father plan their escape to England in the wake of revolution, Lavinia arranges to marry into the titled nobility of England, thereby securing her position in the highest possible class of the highly stratified society. Johnny's infatuation with Lavinia signifies his stubborn connection to his vices. As he matures out of his arrogance and selfishness, Lavinia slowly loses her grip on him. The more that Johnny loses his yearning for petty personal gain, the more Cilla begins to overshadow Lavinia in his mind.

SUMMARY & ANALYSIS

CHAPTER I: UP AND ABOUT

SUMMARY

> *It is all another way of saying—God's way of saying—*
> *that pride goeth before a fall.*
>
> (See QUOTATIONS, p. 49)

Fourteen-year-old Johnny Tremain is a silversmith's apprentice in Revolutionary-era Boston. He lives with an elderly master silversmith, Mr. Lapham, and two other apprentices. Rounding out the bustling household is Mr. Lapham's daughter-in-law and able housekeeper, Mrs. Lapham, and her four daughters.

Johnny has a special status within the Lapham house because he is considered the most talented young silversmith in Boston, and his skill brings in enough money to comfortably support the family. Johnny's time is deemed so valuable that he is not forced to take part in the menial chores that the other two apprentices, eleven-year-old Dusty and sixteen-year-old Dove, are expected to perform. Proud and arrogant, Johnny lets his special position in the household go to his head: he insults the other boys for their clumsy mistakes and orders them around as if they were his servants. Mr. Lapham, a pious Christian, disapproves of Johnny's arrogance. One day at breakfast he asks Johnny to read aloud some Bible verses regarding the sin of pride. Johnny acknowledges the rebuke but fails to rein in his arrogance.

Johnny's relationship with Dove and Dusty is strained, but he is on friendly terms with the four Lapham daughters, particularly the two younger girls, Priscilla and Isannah. Mrs. Lapham wants Johnny to marry one of her daughters so that the silver business will stay within the family when Johnny takes it over. Priscilla, known as Cilla, is considered the most appropriate match, because her two older sisters, Madge and Dorcas, are too old, and the youngest, Isannah, is too sickly. Fourteen-year-old Cilla and Johnny interact primarily through good-natured insults, but these reveal a mutual fondness. The lion's share of Cilla's affection, however, is reserved for the ethereal-looking eight-year-old Isannah, whom Cilla loves and protects with a fierce passion.

In an exciting turn for the Lapham silver shop, the wealthy and powerful merchant John Hancock orders a sugar basin to match an existing tea set. Though Mr. Lapham was the original craftsman of the tea set, he is now old and doubtful that he can duplicate the skill of his youth, and so is reluctant to accept the job. Johnny, eager to work with such a beautiful design, accepts the job on his master's behalf. Johnny struggles to design the handles for the sugar basin, but is continually dissatisfied with his attempts. After one particularly grueling session at the kiln, Cilla approaches Johnny in the middle of the night and asks him to accompany her to the wharf with Isannah. Isannah, she explains, is feeling sick and can only be soothed by the cool, fresh sea air. While they sit alone in the deserted night, Johnny feels intense intimacy with the girls, and reveals a secret he has never before told anyone. He explains that he is related to Jonathan Lyte, a wealthy Boston merchant. Before his mother died, he tells Cilla, she gave him a silver cup marked with the Lyte family coat of arms. Johnny's mother told him to keep the cup hidden and never to approach the Lytes unless he was in serious trouble and had no other recourse. Johnny shows the cup to Cilla, but only after she promises to keep it a secret.

ANALYSIS

Johnny Tremain is not only a coming-of-age story, but also a work of historical fiction that provides a vivid portrayal of pre-Revolutionary Boston. We immediately learn that education was not compulsory in colonial Boston, nor was it common except among the upper classes. Although the literacy rate was higher in the colonies than in England, a person outside the upper class was considered highly educated with only the ability to read, write, and perform simple arithmetic. Johnny is deemed extremely well educated because he can read without stumbling. Unless a child came from a wealthy family, his or her labor was needed to support the family financially. For example, the son of a shopkeeper or a skilled artisan would enter into his father's trade as soon as he was capable of carrying out simple tasks, and a daughter would begin helping her mother with housework as soon as she could walk. Families without a business of their own would pay skilled artisans to take their sons in as apprentices. In return for the valuable training that the apprentice received, for seven years all products of his labor belonged to his master. After those seven years, the apprentice became a master and could set up his own shop.

Johnny Tremain illuminates the characteristics of the institution of marriage in colonial America. The customs regarding marriage were less rigid among the middle and lower classes, but class and economics still heavily affected marriage rituals. For example, Mrs. Lapham is eager to marry one of her daughters to Johnny because, as the most talented apprentice, he will inevitably inherit the silver shop. Whether Johnny actually loves one of her daughters, or any of them love him back, is not really an important consideration in this economic arrangement. Johnny takes it as a matter of course that his mistress wants him to marry one of her daughters, as it is a common occurrence for a good apprentice to marry into his master's family and business.

Religion played an integral role in colonial American society and law. A person could be punished for not observing religious dictums such as the prohibition against working on the Sabbath. However, during the time period of the novel, some of the religious restrictions on colonial society were becoming more relaxed. Near the end of the eighteenth century, the Congregationalist Church of Boston, like all the colonial churches, began losing much of its power over the people. The church's loss of power was the result of many factors, including the increasingly cosmopolitan character of the colonies, a trend toward clerical intellectualism that alienated most laypeople, and a creeping liberalism within lay thought. The downward shift in religious fervor is portrayed nicely in the divide between Mr. Lapham and the younger members of his household. Mr. Lapham's family regards his piety as somewhat old-fashioned. They react to his breakfast Bible readings with amused tolerance, and, in the next chapter, they even violate the Sabbath that he holds so holy.

The pre-Revolutionary world that Johnny lives in is characterized by rapid change and shifting attitudes. While Johnny navigates the precarious obstacles of adolescence, the colonies undergo a similar turbulent coming-of-age. The growing cultural, political, and economic conflicts with Britain throw the colonies into a reckless race to redefine their identities and differentiate themselves from their parent country. Johnny comes into close contact with key figures in the American Revolution, such as John Hancock, Samuel Adams, and Paul Revere, and his coming-of-age coincides with the coming-of-age of their revolutionary ideas. Johnny's maturation is a metaphor for the maturation of the colonies into an independent nation with its own unique politics and culture.

We can see from the very first scene that Johnny's pride is both an obstacle and an asset. His arrogance invites potentially dangerous animosity from those with whom he must work and live. His arrogance also drives him to rash actions, such as his impetuous decision to accept the Hancock order on behalf of his master. However, Johnny's pride also motivates him to work tirelessly. He is not satisfied with anything less than perfection. Johnny is still a child at this point in the story, and his tendencies toward arrogance have yet to solidify into a rigid adult personality. At this point his development can take one of two courses: he can draw on the positive side of his pride to become self- motivated and self-possessed, or he can indulge in the negative aspects of his pride and turn into an arrogant, impetuous man. The story of Johnny's maturation, which is the primary story of the book, is largely the story of how he develops an adult personality during the events of a developing nation.

CHAPTER II: THE PRIDE OF YOUR POWER

SUMMARY

Though everyone assures Johnny that the handle he designed for the sugar bowl is beautiful, Johnny remains unconvinced. Before casting the wax model in silver, he takes his design to Paul Revere, a silversmith of great repute, to ask his advice. Johnny has never met Revere before and is shocked to discover that the great artisan knows his name and his face. Johnny is not aware that all of the master silversmiths in Boston have been watching him. Revere immediately spots the imperfection that Johnny was sensing all along in his design: the curve of the handle is wrong, and the ornate design too large. Revere offers to buy the rest of Johnny's apprentice time from Mr. Lapham for more than the normal price, but Johnny refuses the honor. He explains to Revere that he is the Laphams' chief breadwinner and cannot abandon them.

Back at home, Johnny follows Revere's advice about the sugar bowl, and he is finally satisfied with his work. He quickly makes the wax models and sends Dove to buy some charcoal, but Dove returns with charcoal of inferior quality. Johnny fiercely criticizes Dove, which bothers Mr. Lapham. Mr. Lapham lectures Johnny about his attitude, encouraging him to be more pious. Consequently, he forbids

Johnny to work that evening. Johnny despairs because Mr. Hancock wanted the sugar basin by Monday morning, and it is now Saturday night. Working on Sunday is not only against the law, but it would be a violation of Mr. Lapham's pious lifestyle. Mr. Lapham seems entirely unconcerned by the prospect of failing to meet the deadline.

Mrs. Lapham, however, does not put much stock in her father-in-law's strict religious beliefs and casual attitude toward work, so she urges Johnny to work on Sunday. Mr. Lapham, she points out, will be away most of the day, so he will never know if the religious rule to rest on Sunday is violated. Johnny's work begins well, but Dove deliberately hands him a cracked crucible. Dove's intention is to humble Johnny by making him look clumsy when the silver spills out, but his actions result in a terrible accident. When the crucible breaks, spilling molten silver over the furnace, Johnny slips and badly burns his hand. Mrs. Lapham is afraid to reveal Johnny's sin of breaking the Sabbath, so she summons a midwife instead of a doctor. The midwife does not bandage Johnny's hand correctly, and when the bandages come off, Johnny's thumb is fused to his palm, ruining him forever as a silversmith. Johnny walks through Boston in an angry, bleak mood. The Lapham family's careful courtesy and Dove's impudence infuriate him. When Mr. Lapham learns that Johnny broke the Sabbath to work on the basin, he melts down the entire piece and tells John Hancock that he cannot fill his order, giving no explanation for the failure. Mr. Lapham also discloses to Johnny that Dove was the true cause of his accident and asks him to forgive Dove "like a true Christian." Johnny, however, only swears revenge.

ANALYSIS

Mr. Lapham and Johnny have vastly different attitudes toward work, religion, and humanity, and these divergent opinions may reflect a broad difference between the older and younger colonists. Mr. Lapham has a somewhat laid-back work ethic—he is unconcerned about meeting deadlines and not interested in achieving fame and fortune. He thoroughly enjoys casting silver and feels it is his moral and religious duty to provide for his family. These motivations alone drive his labor. Johnny, on the other hand, is fervently ambitious. He views the Hancock sugar basin order as his chance to achieve widespread recognition, and through that recognition, to build a lucrative silver business. Johnny fantasizes about running a shop outside of his home, which only the most successful silversmiths can afford to do, and he dreams about all the important people who will come to beg for his services. This shift in work ethic is reflected in the difference between the dreams of the older and younger colonists. The older colonists have small dreams: they want to comfortably support their families, work at their trades, and enjoy religious freedom. The younger colonists have more robust dreams, and they desire to get all the money, rights, and opportunities. The younger colonists are not as easily satisfied with their role in life, and their growing needs lead to a broader dissatisfaction with English rule. When the British try to raise revenue from the colonists in the wake of the French and Indian War, taxing them and limiting their self-rule, they threaten the ambitions of the younger generations, who want to maintain control over their pocketbooks and their colonial legislatures. The older generation might have suffered silently under the new impositions, but the new generation protests and ultimately revolts.

Mr. Lapham and Johnny also view religion through different lenses. Mr. Lapham is gravely pious. He reads the Bible more often than he casts silver, and he tries to imbue all actions in his life with the instructions he finds in the Holy Book. Though he constantly urges Johnny to take the advice of the Bible seriously—to rein in his arrogance and to learn to forgive—Johnny is indifferent to these suggestions. The Bible, and religion in general, does not interest Johnny, and he does not use religion as a guide for how he should treat others or live his life. He is not even reluctant to break the Sabbath, which at that time was considered a sin and was against the law. Mr. Lapham's daughter-in-law, Mrs. Lapham, shares Johnny's lax attitude toward the Sabbath, which suggests that the shift in religious attitude is generational. Later on, we see that these lenient attitudes toward religion exist also among the leaders of the revolutionary cause. The leaders meet on Sunday to conduct political business, and the Minute Men train on Sunday.

In part, the more relaxed religious attitudes among the younger generation are the result of the increasingly cosmopolitan character of the colonies. During the time in which the novel is set, Boston is the largest city in the colonies and a major international port. However, the shift in religious attitudes was not limited to the colonies. The eighteenth century brought on a gradual but perceptible weakening of religious observance all over Western Europe. Philosophers who were part of the intellectual movement called the Enlightenment believed that truth lay in science and rational exploration rather than in religion and faith. The new Enlightenment beliefs spread widely and eventually influenced the colonies by way of large port cities like Boston.

The broader shift in European thought is another underlying cause of the younger generation's revolt against England. The Enlightenment's focus on reason rather than faith led to the belief in radical ideas about politics. As thinkers sought to examine all doctrines with their rational faculties, they came to reject many of the traditional doctrines and form new ones. Religious tolerance became more important, as well as the idea of individual rights, or the natural rights that belong to all men, regardless of wealth, class, religion, and race. In England, and all other countries at this time, the small elite ruled over the large masses, masses of people who had no influence in government. A poor man of low class had little control over the direction of his life. The Enlightenment increased people's desire to change the unbalanced power structure, which led to the Founding Fathers' desire to fight for their own country, in which individual rights would be honored.

Johnny and Mr. Lapham approach personal relationships in entirely different ways. Mr. Lapham believes that people should forgive all wrongs and not hold grudges. His attitude toward humanity and morality leads him to be politically apathetic: just as he does not believe in avenging a wrong done by an individual, he does not believe in avenging a wrong done by a government. Mr. Lapham reveals to Johnny that he disapproves of the people who are "trying to stir up discontent in Boston." He would prefer to forgive England for whatever wrongs it has imposed on the colonists, and to continue living a quiet, peaceful life. Johnny, however, takes a much more belligerent stance toward the world. His hostility takes a selfish turn, and he hopes to exact revenge for the wrongs that were done to him personally. For example, Johnny wishes to get revenge on Dove for the foolish prank that resulted in Johnny's injury. But as Johnny matures into a less selfish individual, his belligerence becomes directed toward ideological enemies rather than personal ones, and he develops into a patriot and a soldier.

CHAPTERS III–IV

SUMMARY: CHAPTER III: AN EARTH OF BRASS

Don't touch me! Don't touch me with that dreadful hand!
(See QUOTATIONS, p. 50)

Johnny is unable to earn money and now is just an added expense for the Laphams. Mrs. Lapham begins insulting Johnny the way she once insulted the other boys, and looks at him with uncloaked resentment. She complains about having to feed someone who does not help put food on the table. Cilla begins hiding food in Johnny's pockets so that he does not have to eat in front of Mrs. Lapham. Mr. Lapham assures Johnny that he can remain a part of their household for as long as he needs, but Johnny's pride is severely hurt by his lowered status. Consequently, he dwells in self-pity and longs to find a new home. Unfortunately, as he makes his rounds from artisan to artisan he is consistently rejected because of his crippled hand. Only the butcher offers to take him in, but Johnny cannot bring himself to accept such unskilled work. Meanwhile, Mrs. Lapham begins negotiating a business partnership with an adult silversmith named Mr. Tweedie to ensure that there will be someone to take over the shop when Mr. Lapham dies. Johnny resents Mr. Tweedie for usurping a position that was once his, and when they run into each other one day at the Lapham house, Johnny viciously attacks Tweedie with a barrage of insults and accusations, earning himself another enemy.

While in search of work, Johnny enters the print shop of the *Boston Observer,* a Whig newspaper. The quiet, dark, older boy minding the shop sizes Johnny up silently and offers him something to eat. Johnny is drawn to the boy, who introduces himself as Rab, and finds himself sharing the story of his accident, the Laphams, and his search for a new trade. Rab offers Johnny a job delivering the *Observer,* but Johnny still hopes to find skilled labor as an artisan. Rab kindly tells him to return if he can find nothing else.

Johnny next approaches John Hancock for a job. Hancock does not recognize Johnny as the silversmith who was supposed to make his basin, but Johnny's quantitative skills impress Hancock so much that he prepares to take him in as a clerk. However, he rescinds the offer when sees Johnny's handwriting, which is illegible because of his injury. Hancock sends Johnny away, but later sends his slave boy to give him a bag of silver. Johnny wastes this small windfall on expensive foods, and he is ashamed by his lack of prudence, reflecting that Rab would never act so foolishly. With the remainder of his money, he purchases new shoes for himself and spends the rest on gifts for Isannah and Cilla. When Johnny returns home, Mrs. Lapham accuses him of stealing the new shoes he is wearing, but she cannot ruin his good mood. Cilla and Isannah are delighted with their gifts, but when Johnny tries to pick up Isannah, she declares that she does not want him to touch her with his "dreadful hand." Heartbroken, Johnny cries himself to sleep on his mother's unmarked grave. He decides that he has finally hit rock bottom and the time has come to approach Jonathan Lyte.

SUMMARY: CHAPTER IV: THE RISING EYE

Lyte thinks that Johnny is a conniving impostor, but Johnny announces that he can prove his story with a silver cup bearing the Lyte seal. Lyte urges Johnny to bring the cup to his house that evening. On his way to the Lyte home, Johnny stops by the *Observer* to tell Rab what happened. Rab warns that Lyte is a crooked man who pretends to be a loyal British citizen when dealing with Tories and pretends to be sympathetic to the rebel cause when dealing with Whigs. He loans Johnny a fine linen shirt and corduroy jacket. When Johnny returns to Lyte and presents the cup, Lyte accuses him of theft. Lyte announces to his houseguests that he once owned four such cups, but that one was stolen on August 23. Mrs. Lapham, he continues, has already sworn that Johnny never owned such a cup and has confided in Lyte her suspicion that Johnny has resorted to crime. Mr. Tweedie has further offered that Johnny is a known liar. Based on this evidence assembled by Lyte, the sheriff places Johnny under arrest.

Rab visits Johnny in jail. Johnny stays in a comfortable, private cell because the jailor, the turnkey, and Rab are all members of the Sons of Liberty, a semisecret, slightly violent organization that tries to resist the alleged tyranny of Britain. Rab asks Johnny whether anyone saw the cup in his possession prior to August 23, and Johnny remembers that he showed the cup to Cilla in early July. Later, Rab discovers that Lyte is attempting to block Cilla's testimony in court by bribing the Laphams with a big silver order and a promise of further orders should they cooperate. Mrs. Lapham forbids Cilla from testifying, but Rab attests that he will find a way to sneak her to court on the day of the trial. Rab also secures a lawyer for Johnny, the famous Whig attorney Josiah Quincy, who agrees to defend Johnny free of charge.

At the trial, Rab appears with Cilla as planned. Afterward, he reveals how he accomplished this feat: he presented Mrs. Lapham with a letter bearing the seal of the governor. Though the letter bore no relation to the trial, the illiterate Mrs. Lapham had no way of knowing this. Cilla testifies that she saw the cup in early July. Isannah repeats Cilla's testimony, although she herself did not actually see the cup and is merely mimicking her older sister. Convinced by the testimony of the two girls, the judge rules that Johnny is innocent and orders that his cup be returned to him. After the trial, the famous beauty Lavinia Lyte, daughter of Jonathan Lyte and the object of Johnny's reluctant infatuation, seems drawn to Isannah, taking her hand and remarking on her ethereal beauty. Isannah kisses Johnny's burned hand before they leave the courtroom, restoring his spirits.

ANALYSIS: CHAPTERS III–IV

After reading Chapter III, we may feel pity for Johnny and surprise at Mrs. Lapham's actions. Her grim attitude toward Johnny after his accident appears cruel and insensitive. However, as the mistress of a household that does not have a steady source of income, she does not have the luxury of letting Johnny wallow in self-pity. Johnny has become a financial burden on her family, and the other apprentices are untalented and unable to pull in enough money to feed a family of nine. Therefore, Johnny's accident is not just a major setback for Johnny, but for the entire Lapham family. Though Mr. Lapham seems to treat Johnny favorably in contrast to Mrs. Lapham, we must remember that it is Mrs. Lapham's duty to feed and clothe a large household. Mrs. Lapham is a resourceful and practical woman, whose first interest lies in providing for her family.

With his secure, quiet confidence, Rab serves as a foil to Johnny, who is quick-tempered, talkative, and insecure. Sensitive and understanding, Rab offers Johnny a patient ear and food because he senses right away that Johnny is too proud to ask for either. In return, Johnny immediately looks up to Rab as a role model. For example, when Johnny wastefully spends the majority of his silver from Hancock on a lavish feast, he asks himself whether Rab would have done the same. Johnny acknowledges that his decision to spend the money on a feast is a foolish one, because Rab would not have spent the money that way. Johnny's acquaintance with Rab marks the beginning of his transformation from a selfish child to a selfless and patriotic man. Johnny will accomplish such a transformation by emulating Rab's actions and seeing the world through Rab's eyes.

Jonathan Lyte also serves as a foil to Johnny. His arrogantly flippant reaction to Johnny's claims of kinship reminds us of Johnny's arrogant pride, suggesting that the arrogance is hereditary. Johnny, however, is still a child, and we do not know whether his vanity will change into noble pride or petty arrogance. Jonathan Lyte represents one path that Johnny can take, where selfish arrogance takes the form of cruelty and crookedness. Forbes introduces Rab and Lyte concurrently, showing the strong contrast between the two characters. Johnny can either mature into a man with Rab's quiet confidence or a man with Lyte's cruel vanity. Johnny's decision to use his small windfall from Hancock to purchase gifts for Isannah and Cilla demonstrates that he has the capacity for generous behavior. His selfless act is an indication that, given the right environment and influences, he can change in a positive direction and may well avoid the fate that Lyte embodies.

Johnny's struggle with Lyte foreshadows the coming battle between Britain and the colonies. Johnny, like the colonies, does not have resources to fight, but he finds himself at war with a wealthy, well-equipped opponent. Johnny enters this battle because of his desire to assert himself as an equal of the rich and powerful Lyte; he wants to enjoy the privileges of the Lytes and those in the wealthy class. Similarly, the colonists struggle against the British because they want all people to be treated as equals so that everyone can enjoy the same privileges. Social and economic class is an important motif throughout the Lyte-Tremain struggle, just as it was an important motif in the ideology of the colonial rebels. Lyte insults Johnny primarily by mocking his poverty and his ancestry, attacking him based on his social and economic class. Like the colonists, Johnny the underdog ultimately triumphs against his powerful enemy.

CHAPTER V: *THE BOSTON OBSERVER*

SUMMARY

Johnny is still desperately trying to find a job, so he decides to sell his silver cup for money to tide him over. He believes that he can ask the highest price from Lyte, since Lyte would want the cup to round out his set. When Johnny approaches Lyte, however, the crooked older man tries to have Johnny arrested again by claiming that Johnny has just confessed to him. Lyte's elderly clerks agree to testify that Johnny privately confessed his crime. Johnny hurls insults at Lyte before frantically fleeing arrest.

Johnny returns to the *Observer* and asks if there is still a position available. On Rab's recommendation, Uncle Lorne, the owner of the print shop, hires Johnny on the spot. Rab offers to share his living quarters above the print shop with Johnny. To deliver newspapers, Johnny must learn to ride a horse. Unfortunately, the only horse the newspaper owns is Goblin, who is beautiful but extremely timid, and therefore difficult to ride. Rab gives Johnny one riding lesson and then leaves him to learn on his own. In almost no time, and with no help, Johnny expertly learns to ride the nervous horse. When Lorne praises Johnny for this near-impossible feat, Johnny uncharacteristically hides his pleasure, because he thinks that Rab would behave the same way.

Riding Goblin forces Johnny to use his crippled hand, so he is no longer worried that his right hand will atrophy from lack of use. Johnny learns to write with his left hand, because Rab gives him papers to copy, taking it for granted that Johnny will find a way to copy them. To earn extra money, Johnny begins delivering letters, but Johnny uses most of his free time reading the books in Mr. Lorne's ample library. Mrs. Lorne, Rab's aunt, sometimes asks Johnny to watch her baby, and Johnny begins to feel a strong attachment to the child. He attempts to hide his tender feelings, but Mrs. Lorne can see through his scornful exterior to his sweet and lonely true self, and she treats Johnny like a son. As a part of the Lorne household, Johnny quickly becomes an ardent Whig. Not only is the *Boston Observer* a rabid Whig paper, but the Boston Observers, a powerful secret club dedicated to resolving issues of British tyranny, holds its meetings in Johnny and Rab's loft, and the two boys are often allowed to sit in on their meetings.

Johnny continues to model his behavior on Rab's example and explicit advice. When Rab suggests that Johnny try to tame his temper, Johnny vows not to act so rashly. Soon afterward, Samuel Adams's slave accidentally splashes dishwater on Johnny, and he suppresses his natural instinct to lash out angrily. The slave girl apologizes profusely and dries Johnny's clothes, while he eats some of her apple pie. As a result, Adams treats Johnny as an equal and hires him to ride for the important Boston Committee of Correspondence, which will later become the Continental Congress.

Johnny runs into Cilla and Isannah at the water pump one day. He is surprised by how little he has missed the girls who were once his two best friends, and he thinks about how much he loves his new life and his new best friend, Rab. Johnny's one complaint is that Rab is too self-contained and refuses to divulge any personal information or be influenced by others. Johnny promises to meet the girls at the pump every Thursday and Sunday, but then he fails to keep his promise.

On two occasions, Johnny sees Rab veer from his normally taciturn manner. First, at a party, Johnny sees Rab become wildly animated as he dances with all the girls. The next time he sees Rab similarly animated is during a fight. The local butcher's son bullies Uncle Lorne's young apprentices, the Webb twins, and Rab and Johnny fight to rescue the twins and their cat. Johnny observes that on certain occasions, such as when he is dancing at a party, people fail to notice his crippled hand. Rab explains that people only notice the hand when Johnny draws attention to it.

ANALYSIS

As Johnny finds meaningful activities to fill his time and his thoughts, his injury becomes less important to him and to the plot of the novel. The narrator hardly talks about Johnny's handicap in these chapters, except to mention that the hand is not bothering him. Johnny's work, reading, and riding leave him little time to brood over his misfortune. Once he stops worrying about his hand, its physical condition starts to improve. Johnny unknowingly saves his hand from atrophy by using it while he rides instead of hiding it away in shame. He manages to resume all of his old activities, like writing, and even picks up new ones, like dancing, by realizing that, with effort, he can overcome his disability.

Rab insightfully points out that whenever Johnny stops fixating on his handicap, no one else seems to notice it either. In other words, Johnny's attitude toward his hand affects the way other people react to it. This seems to be true not only of his physical handicap but of his psychological one as well. As Johnny ceases to wallow in childish self-pity and selfish anger, the people around him stop treating him like a child and start treating him as a trusted confidant. Under Rab's influence, and with the emotional support of a caring family, Johnny learns the value of modesty, quiet confidence, and patience. The Whig leaders of Boston notice these qualities and induct Johnny into their underground operations. Johnny views himself as a young man rather than a boy, and, as a result, the leaders trust him with the secret knowledge of a colonial conspiracy.

By attending the meetings of the Boston Observers, and through his reading in Mr. Lorne's library, Johnny is becoming acquainted with the philosophy behind the political turmoil in Boston. Before, he was a Whig simply because Rab and Mr. Lorne were Whigs, but now he is intellectually convinced. Johnny's Whig allegiance transforms from a personal, emotional attachment to a political and ideological stance. This change also signals Johnny's emergence from childhood to manhood. At first, a child's loyalties are forged purely out of familiarity or habit, and emotion. Ideally, a man gives his allegiance to groups and ideas that he believes in rationally.

The Enlightenment philosophy behind the revolutionary sentiment is based on the idea of the natural rights of man: each human being has the same rights, regardless of class, religion, or race. Ironically, many of the prominent leaders of the American Revolution who advocated the natural rights of man also owned slaves. Esther Forbes does not hide this fact, and slaves belonging to John Hancock and Samuel Adams appear in the novel. Many leaders of the American Revolution were uncomfortable with the hypocrisy of preaching against English tyranny while owning slaves. Others, however, did not even recognize their hypocrisy, much less feel guilty about it. During the colonial period, the rational ideals of the Enlightenment did not change all of people's deeply ingrained cultural and racial biases. Only in later decades was the rhetoric of human rights extended to include people of all races and both genders.

Slaves were a tragic exception to what was otherwise a strikingly egalitarian society, although women also did not have rights. Almost all white American males, and even some free black men, were farmers with small plots of land. In the cities there was a growing class of skilled artisans, like Mr. Lapham and Paul Revere, as well as an emerging class of wealthy merchants, like Hancock and Lyte, who had become wealthy during the armed conflicts of the 1690s and early 1770s. While this latter group frightened some colonists with the prospect of the "Europeanization" of America, the colonies did not have a ruling nobility or a pauper underclass. In America, social stratification was minimal, and social mobility was high. Unlike in England, it was relatively easy for an ambitious farmer or servant to rise to a position of wealth and influence.

CHAPTERS VI–VII

SUMMARY: CHAPTER VI: SALT-WATER TEA

> *That worst of Plagues, the detested tea shipped for this*
> *Port by the East India Company, is now arrived in the*
> *Harbour: the hour of destruction, of manly opposition*
> *to the machinations of Tyranny, stares you in the face.*
> (See QUOTATIONS, p. 51)

Many American colonists, most notably Johnny's powerful new
Whig friends, resent the fact that England levies taxes on them without allowing them to represent themselves in government. Therefore, when England sends a shipment of tea with a small tax
attached, the Boston Observers schedule a meeting to discuss their
next steps. Johnny goes to the house of each member, giving the
summons for the meeting, which is encoded as a newspaper bill.
Josiah Quincy and John Adams prevent Johnny from notifying
James Otis about the meeting, even though he is the founder of the
organization, because Otis is mentally unstable. When Johnny
informs Doctor Warren of the meeting, the kind physician asks
Johnny if he can examine his hand, but Johnny refuses. Meanwhile,
the Sons of Liberty post placards calling for opposition to the shipment of tea. Johnny is excited by the hubbub, but when a Whig mob
brutally beats a Tory right outside the *Observer* shop, he feels sick
and frightened.

At the meeting, the Observers decide to the dump the offending
tea into Boston Harbor if the governor refuses to send the ships back
to London. Rab is asked to recruit trustworthy boys for the mission
but is asked to keep the mission a secret. Johnny asks Rab if he will
be included in this trusted group of boys. Rab responds by telling
Johnny to practice chopping logs so that he will be able to chop tea
chests when the time comes. The governor refuses to send the ships
back to London, and the Boston Tea Party takes place as planned.
Johnny and the other participants dress up as Native Americans,
board the ships at night, chop open chests of tea, and toss the con-
tents into the Boston Harbor. Johnny notices Dove among the participants. Instead of throwing the tea overboard, Dove is stealing
tea, thereby undermining the moral high ground of the political pro-
testers. As punishment, Rab tosses Dove into the water.

SUMMARY: CHAPTER VII: THE FIDDLER'S BILL

Only that a man can stand up.

(See QUOTATIONS, p. 52)

England closes the port of Boston until the colonists pay for the tea, and British soldiers occupy the city. Commerce grinds to a halt, but the city refuses to be starved into submission. Lorne and other printers continue to print Whig papers despite the danger of treason charges. Local militias form and begin drilling with old, worn-out firearms. Many of the British soldiers sympathize with the colonists, and many others would prefer to be with their families than in Boston. Meanwhile, other colonies send shipments of food by land to ensure that Boston does not starve.

Johnny enters Lorne's shop one afternoon to find Cilla doing a sketch for the *Observer*. Her easy manner with Rab makes him intensely jealous. Cilla reports that Lavinia, Lyte's daughter, became so enchanted with Isannah that she requested that the child live with her. Mrs. Lapham was happy to oblige, but Isannah refused to go without Cilla. Thus, Cilla now works as a servant in the Lyte house, while Lavinia parades Isannah around Boston high society like a prized pet. Johnny asks Cilla if he can see her when he delivers the *Observer* to the Lytes. Cilla is noncommittal in her response. Rab walks her home, much to Johnny's dismay.

Johnny discovers that Dove is working as a stable boy for the English Colonel Smith. The British stable boys entertain themselves by bullying Dove. Although Johnny does not like Dove, he protects him when he can. His old hatred for Dove has disappeared, as has his resentment of his other old enemies. As an act of goodwill, he hires Mr. Tweedie to mend his riding spurs. While at the Lapham home, he discovers that Madge has fallen in love with a British sergeant named Gale.

Colonel Smith's assistant, Lieutenant Stranger, tries to commandeer Goblin for his boss. Johnny lets the lieutenant ride Goblin. Meanwhile, Johnny helps Lydia, the black washerwoman, hang some sheets. He and Lydia let a sheet flap in the wind to frighten Goblin. Goblin throws Stranger, so Johnny gets to keep his horse. Stranger respects Johnny's love for Goblin as well as his cleverness, so he offers to teach him to jump hurdles. Johnny's stunt also wins the respect of the British stable boys, who help Johnny find food for Goblin when supplies run low.

Johnny occasionally visits Cilla at the Lyte family mansion. It bothers him that Lavinia's attention has gone to Isannah's head, but it bothers him more to see Cilla treated like a common servant. Mrs. Bessie, the Lyte's cook and Cilla's new best friend, is an ardent Whig and a secret ally of Samuel Adams. She tells Johnny that the Sons of Liberty plan to tar and feather the Lytes at their country home, but she promises to protect Cilla and Isannah.

ANALYSIS: CHAPTERS VI–VII

As the rebel colonial forces begin to mobilize, resorting to action instead of just words, Johnny grapples with the complex morality of violent political protest. We see in these chapters that mob violence, rational political theory, and exuberant optimism all drive the Revolutionary fervor in colonial Boston. Whigs engage in acts of random violence, such as tarring and feathering Tory families, as well as in controlled acts of violence under the guise of political protests like the Boston Tea Party. Though Johnny believes in the political rhetoric behind such acts as the Boston Tea Party and the harassment of Tories, he is not convinced that lofty ends justify the violent means. Johnny does not actually examine the issues of Whig violence in an explicit, intellectual way. He is excited by the rational, idealistic underpinnings of rebellion, but sickened by the fact that human beings must be harmed, or even killed, to implement these rebellious ideas. Violence, however, particularly mob violence, is the only tool available to the Whig colonists, who wield no other power over England. Nearly a decade of fruitless boycotts and diplomatic political agitation has taught them that nonviolent means are not sufficient for their end.

In response to the Boston Tea Party, the British government passed a series of legislations known in the colonies as the Intolerable Acts. The Intolerable Acts not only ordered that the port of Boston be closed until all the tea was paid for, they also dictated that British officials accused of violence be tried in English rather than American courts, that British troops could be quartered in any town in Massachusetts, and that the Massachusetts charter be amended to greatly reduce the colony's right to self-government. We see in Chapter VII that outrage over these acts spread far beyond Massachusetts, uniting the thirteen colonies for the first time. Not only did the other colonies provide Boston with food and other provisions, but also the leaders of other colonies began to seriously discuss a plan for a unified secession from Britain.

When the British forces occupy Boston, the idea of war and enemies becomes confusing for Johnny, as it does for many colonists.
Though the colonial population resents the ruling British, there is
little resentment toward the actual British troops. In fact, many
colonials are friends with the British soldiers, as in the case of
Johnny's friendship with Lieutenant Stranger or the romance
between Madge Lapham and Sergeant Gale. The soldiers are gener-
ally well behaved and not intrusive. In addition, apart from the
officers, they are mostly poor boys who are no better represented in
Parliament than the colonists. There is still the sense that the soldiers and the colonists belong to the same group, since the colonists
thought of themselves as British citizens, and even intense political
conflict could not shatter their cultural identity.

The tensions between the British soldiers and the colonists serve
to illustrate the origins of many of our country's most fundamental
laws. The British harass Mr. Lorne and other printers of rebellious
newspapers, threatening to hang them if they do not cease their
seditious propagandizing. The desire of the colonists to voice protests gave rise to the constitutionally protected rights to free speech
and freedom of the press. The anger over taxation without political
representation led to a government based on democratically elected
lawmakers. The constitutionally protected right to bear arms originated in the colonists' mad scramble to create a fighting force to
oppose the well-equipped, better-prepared British troops. In creating their ideal society from scratch, the creators of the new government drew heavily on the recent grievances they suffered under
British rule, seeking to outlaw such grievances for the future.

The character of Lydia, the black washerwoman, highlights an
often ignored and marginalized portion of the American Revolutionary movement—black Americans. While it is ironic that many
of the architects of the American Revolution were also slave own-
ers, it is equally remarkable that free American blacks and slaves
also participated in the rebel cause despite their lower status in the
colonies. The British often ignored or discounted slaves as a threat,
so people such as Lydia were able to serve effectively as spies. The
slaves' position as servants within the inns and homes that the British officers occupied made them ideal for this crucial work. Freed
blacks and slaves also served as Minute Men, and gave their lives
for American independence. Sadly, despite their aid in the war for
American independence, they would not win their own independence for nearly another century.

CHAPTERS VIII–IX

SUMMARY: CHAPTER VIII: A WORLD TO COME

Mrs. Bessie warns the Lytes just before the Whig mob comes for them because she cannot bear to see them treated roughly. The Lytes escape from their country house and head toward Boston with only the clothing on their backs. Jonathan Lyte has an anxiety attack due to the scare, so Doctor Warren instructs Lavinia to keep him away from stress. Cilla and Johnny borrow Doctor Warren's carriage and horse so they can return to the Lytes' country house to fetch the precious silver left behind in the hasty departure. While in the house, Johnny pockets Jonathan Lyte's important papers hoping that they will be of interest to Samuel Adams. He also finds a family genealogy in an old Bible and discovers that his mother's name is scratched out. The genealogy states that she married a man named Charles Latour and that they both died of plague in Marseilles before the date of Johnny's birth. He cuts out the genealogy, only to burn it a few moments later. Cilla suggests that he seize the opportunity to retrieve his cup from among the Lyte's silver, but Johnny no longer wants any connection to the Lytes and leaves the valuable cup behind.

Rab is caught trying to buy a gun from a farmer who resells British muskets. The British soldiers tar and feather the farmer, but Rab is not punished because he is so young. Meanwhile, Johnny finds it difficult to think of the British as targets rather than people. Madge elopes with Sergeant Gale, so Mrs. Lapham herself marries Mr. Tweedie to keep the silver shop in the family. Johnny learns that Rab has been earnestly courting Cilla, but Cilla finally decides that she likes Johnny best. Johnny admits to himself that he likes her too.

The Observers hold their last meeting because they cannot risk the chance of being discovered. James Otis is not notified, but he arrives and delivers a rousing speech. He declares that they are fighting the British so that "a man can stand up," meaning that they are fighting for the rights of all individuals, everywhere.

SUMMARY: CHAPTER IX: THE SCARLET DELUGE

Paul Revere organizes a spy system made up of master artisans and their apprentices to keep a watch on the British forces in Boston. The purpose of the spy system is to alert any outlying towns if the soldiers appear to be advancing in their direction.

Lydia gives Johnny the shreds of some aborted letters that Lieutenant Stranger had drafted to Lavinia Lyte. The letters reveal valuable information about the movements of British troops. As a result
of this information, the Whig forces are able to seize a store of British
military supplies. Meanwhile, Stranger gives Johnny a lesson jump-
ing hurdles. Johnny is puzzled that Stranger treats him like an equal
where horses are concerned but as an inferior in all other contexts.

Johnny discovers that many of the British regulars are actually
Whigs. One of them, Pumpkin, asks for Johnny's help in deserting
his post. He dreams of owning his own farm, a dream he has no
chance of fulfilling in England. Johnny gives Pumpkin a farmer's
smock sewn by his mother before she died and arranges to have him
smuggled out of Boston. In return, Pumpkin gives Johnny his musket and his old uniform. Johnny gives the musket to Rab. Pumpkin
is caught and executed for desertion by the British.

ANALYSIS: CHAPTERS VIII–IX

Johnny's decision not to retrieve his stolen cup from Lyte is highly significant. The silver cup, a luxury item bearing the seal of a powerful
and wealthy family, is symbolic on two levels. First, the cup symbolizes Johnny's initial vices—his self-centered desires for money, status,
and recognition. The cup is Johnny's only connection to the Lyte family, and the Lyte family, presumably, is the genetic source of his vices,
since the Lytes seem to exhibit the worst aspects of Johnny's personality. When Lyte steals the cup from Johnny, he takes away Johnny's
connection to the Lyte family and the vices that they represent. Cut
off from his sole possession and his only relatives, Johnny must turn
to Rab for help. Modeling Rab's behavior is what ultimately saves
Johnny from his vices, as Rab and his friends transform Johnny into
a selfless patriot. When Johnny passes up the opportunity to take
back his cup from Lyte's possession, he shows that his former selfish,
materialistic ambitions are not important to him anymore.

We can also view the silver cup as a symbol of England and the
type of world that fosters the vices Johnny now rejects. First, the cup
literally originated in England. Second, the cup is a luxury item that
symbolizes Britain's wealth, and its Lyte seal represents Britain's
power and class-consciousness. By leaving behind the cup, Johnny
not only renounces his selfish younger self, he also severs his ties to
England and the system of class and wealth that it fosters. In other words,
Johnny is declaring himself a citizen of America and not of England.

JOHNNY TREMAIN ♦ 41

Johnny's growing awareness of his romantic feelings for Cilla also indicates a final step in his embrace of a new, more democratic, identity. Until this time, Johnny has harbored a slight infatuation with the regally beautiful Lavinia Lyte. Lavinia, with her haughty, noble beauty and her strong preference for London, signifies, like the cup, the old, class-conscious world of England, where nobility of birth is more important than nobility of spirit. When Johnny is focused on his old desires for Lavinia, it is difficult for him to notice Cilla, who, with her unassuming prettiness and self-sacrificing, hardworking, democratic nature, symbolizes the spirit of the colonial rebels. As Johnny loses his yearning for petty personal gain, Lavinia's glamour loses its hold on him, and Cilla's sincere affection becomes more appealing.

It is also significant that Johnny first becomes aware of his feelings for Cilla when Rab begins courting her. Rab is instinctively drawn to nobler, more democratic ideologies, ways of life, and women. Johnny merely follows Rab's lead and models his behavior. At this point in the novel, Johnny is not entirely capable of finding his own path; he still follows Rab, as he struggles toward his new sense of self.

Johnny's relationship with Stranger illustrates the growing cultural divide between Britain and the colonies. Stranger, a British soldier, strictly observes the rules regarding class boundaries in his interactions with Johnny. In the colonies, however, class boundaries are not clear. In Britain, class is a set of rigid norms that delineate possible relationships and ambitions. In the colonies, class is a more fluid demarcation that affects, but does not determine, one's station in life. Stranger's behavior toward Johnny—the way he treats him as a subordinate despite their growing friendship—puzzles the American boy, who is not used to such treatment. The episode with Pumpkin further illustrates the differences between the British and American conceptions of class. Pumpkin longs to desert the army and become an American, because only in the colonies can a poor boy of low class hope to aspire above his station and acquire his own land. America is a land of opportunity and equality, at least compared to England.

Johnny has been growing increasingly aware of the very real and weighty significance of his friends' ideologies, but it is not until he sees Pumpkin killed that Johnny realizes the consequences of violent, armed conflict. Only then does he recognize that his closest friends might die while trying to implement their ideas. Johnny's

SUMMARY & ANALYSIS

fear that Rab will die becomes a small obsession for Johnny for the remainder of the book, manifesting itself in a recurring vision of muskets staring at his friend as if they were the "very eyes of death." The recurring image of the muskets foreshadows Rab's demise on the battlefield.

CHAPTER X: 'DISPERSE, YE REBELS!'

SUMMARY

In April, the Whigs sense that the British are planning to take some military action. Paul Revere and Doctor Warren arrange to warn the outlying Massachusetts towns of the British troops' movements by using lantern signals from the spire of Christ's Church. While Johnny listens to Revere and Warren hash out their plan, he drifts off to sleep and has a frightening dream. In his dream he sees himself boiling lobsters with human eyes and beside him are John Hancock and Samuel Adams. Hancock looks away, pitying the pleading lobster eyes, but Adams relishes every moment. That evening Revere leaves by horse to spread the warning throughout the countryside that the British troops might advance.

Rab is convinced that fighting will break out before the week is over, so he also leaves Boston to report for duty in Lexington. He explains to Johnny that once fighting begins, the British will not allow any man to leave the city of Boston for fear that he will join the rebel forces. Rab seems to feel no grief and only excitement about leaving, but Johnny is devastated by his friend's departure. Johnny offers to accompany Rab to Lexington, but Rab gently reminds him that he is more useful as a spy in Boston than as a soldier who cannot shoot a gun.

Johnny takes his job as a spy seriously, and he spends all day hanging around the Afric Queen, the inn where Colonel Smith sleeps. On April 18, two days after Rab leaves Boston, Dove lets slip that Colonel Smith asked him to polish his campaign saddle rather than his usual saddle. By subtly prodding Dove, Johnny pieces together enough information to surmise that the British are planning an expedition to Lexington and Concord. He runs to give this news to Doctor Warren. Doctor Warren sends Johnny out into the soldier-filled streets to repeat this message to the various players in the elaborate relay system. First Johnny alerts Billy Dawes, who will ride across land to warn the rebels in Lexington and Concord.

Next, he alerts Paul Revere who will travel to the same towns by way of the Charles River. Finally, he summons the parson and instructs him to hang two lanterns in the spire of Christ Church.

When Johnny returns to Warren's place, Revere and Dawes are in the doorway. Revere is urging Warren to accompany him across the Charles River. Once the fighting begins, they assume that the English soldiers will round up colonists suspected of treason and hang them. Warren, however, wants to stay in Boston and keep watch on the British movement until the last possible minute. At dawn on April 19, while Johnny sleeps in Doctor Warren's place, the first shots of war are fired on Lexington Green.

ANALYSIS

Rab's departure is cataclysmic for Johnny because it forces him to reevaluate his own identity and his relationship with Rab. Until now, he has not been forced to think for himself and instead has depended on Rab for guidance and support. Without Rab, Johnny must become his own man: instead of modeling his behavior after Rab's, he must use his own thoughts and ideas. Rab's casual attitude as they part ways hurts Johnny by reminding him how unequal the relationship has been all along: Johnny has always needed Rab, but Rab has never needed Johnny. Rab, as Johnny noted soon after they first became friends, is self-contained—he knows who he is and how he wants to behave. However, Rab's self-containment reminds Johnny of his own lack of a strong identity, and also reminds him that he will never be as important to Rab as Rab is to him.

Johnny's dream about boiling lobsters with human eyes highlights his personal feelings about the conflict between the British and the colonists. He feels pity for the British soldiers, known as "lobsterbacks" because of their red uniforms, and is unable to think of them as merely enemy targets. However, because his best friend is in a precarious position as a Minute Man in Lexington, it seems strange that Johnny is dreaming of dying British soldiers instead of dying colonists. Perhaps the idea of Rab's death is too frightening for Johnny to think about directly, so instead he contemplates the deaths of Rab's battlefield enemies.

Johnny's dream also draws attention to the different attitudes toward and motivations for war among the major Whig players. While Hancock seems to view war as a necessary evil on the path to independence, Johnny suspects that Adams wants war for the sake of war. Hancock, like Otis in his rousing speech, has lofty ideals at the heart of his rebelliousness. Adams, the dream suggests, might simply have revenge in mind when planning the war. In fact, Adams did have very personal reasons for disliking the British. His father had been a principal stockholder of the Land Bank organized in Massachusetts in 1740, and when the British Parliament destroyed the bank, his father was financially ruined. In addition, Adams's personal history suggests that he was a born agitator, always eager for controversy and conflict. Adams's rebelliousness might derive from the sort of petty pride and quick temper that once motivated Johnny to swear revenge on Dove. Supporting this suggestion are Otis's parting words to Adams at the last meeting of the Boston Observers. "You'll play your part," Otis tells Adams scornfully, "but what it is really about . . . you'll never know." Otis clearly insinuates that Adams is an integral part of the revolution, but does not really know what the Americans are fighting for—namely, freedom, independence, and choice.

Finally, Johnny's dream explores the complex moral situation concerning the sacrifice of lives for individual rights. The lobsters look up with their pitiful eyes, wanting their lives to be spared. The lobsters have done nothing wrong, but are being sacrificed to satisfy the hunger of Adams and Hancock. Similarly, the British soldiers have caused no offense to the colonists, but they will be killed because of a war started by the rebel leaders. Hancock may have loftier reasons for starting a war, but it is debatable whether his motives justify the loss of thousands of British and colonial lives. It seems almost hypocritical to sacrifice so many individual lives to achieve individual rights for all.

CHAPTERS XI–XII

SUMMARY: CHAPTER XI: YANKEE DOODLE

> *The cow that lowed, the man who milked, the chickens*
> *that came running and the woman who called them,*
> *the fragrance streaming from the plowed land and the*
> *plowman. These he possessed.*
>
> (See QUOTATIONS, p. 53)

When Johnny wakes up, Doctor Warren tells him about the events that occurred in Lexington. A handful of rebels were killed, but Doctor Warren does not know their names. Johnny instantly thinks about

Rab. Doctor Warren heads to Lexington to tend to the wounded, and Johnny asks to come along. The doctor tells him to stay in Boston and spend the day collecting information, then slip out across the Charles at night to find him and relay what he has gathered.

Outside in the streets of Boston, no one knows that the fighting has begun, but the entire city is at the harbor watching the British soldiers line up and pile into boats. General Gage orders that the leaders of the colonial opposition be arrested, but all of the principal men, such as Adams, Hancock, Revere, and Warren, have already fled toward the fighting in the countryside. Johnny sends a warning message to Uncle Lorne, because printers of Whig papers are also being rounded up. When Johnny finally makes it to the Lorne house, he finds Mrs. Lorne mending a feather mattress. Uncle Lorne steps out of the mattress, and explains that he hid inside because he did not have time to escape.

Next, Johnny goes to the Lyte house. He finds the Lytes loading their possessions into coaches, and he learns that they are moving to London now that war has broken out. Only Cilla and Mrs. Bessie are staying behind. While Johnny talks to Cilla, Lavinia approaches and informs them that Isannah is accompanying her to London. Cilla begs her sister to stay behind. Lavinia asks Isannah if she would prefer a life of luxury or one of poverty. Faced with the choice between her sister and her patroness, Isannah bursts into tears but then quickly chooses to go to London, where Lavinia plans to train the child as an actress.

Lavinia then dismisses Cilla and Mrs. Bessie from the room. She reveals to Johnny that her father was not completely honest when he testified that only four of the six silver cups came to the New World, when in fact, there had been five. Mr. Lyte had no reason to believe, she explains, that Johnny could be in possession of the fifth cup, because he had never been told that Johnny's mother had a child. The entire family believed that both of Johnny's parents died of cholera in France. Johnny's father was a French soldier who became a prisoner of war in Boston during the French and Indian War, and during that time he went under the assumed name of Charles Latour. Johnny's mother fell in love with Charles and defied her parents by running off to France with him after his release. When Charles died, the Tremain family sent his young widow to a convent, hoping that she would convert to Catholicism. It was in that convent that Johnny was born. Lavinia excuses her father's dishonest conduct by swearing that he did not know any of this information at the time of the trial. It was only after the trial that she began to investigate, and uncovered the facts that she is now revealing. Lavinia and her father now acknowledge that Johnny has a right to some of their property, and she tells him that he is free to stake his claim to whatever is left when the war is over.

SUMMARY: CHAPTER XII: A MAN CAN STAND UP
Johnny travels to Lexington, trying to find Doctor Warren, but also searching for news about Rab. When he finds Warren, he learns that Rab was seriously wounded in the first volley of shots fired at Lexington, and he goes to a small back room in a tavern where Rab is resting. Rab gives Johnny his musket, saying that his only regret is that it was never fired in battle. Then he sends Johnny away, asking him to locate his family. No members of Rab's family are in their house, and Johnny returns, defeated, to learn that Rab has died in his absence. Rab had sent him away on a wild-goose chase because he did not want Johnny to see him die.

Alone with Doctor Warren, Johnny finally lets him examine his injured hand. The thumb, the doctor discovers, is fused to the palm only by scar tissue. If Johnny is brave enough to stand the pain, Warren can cut the thumb loose. It is unlikely that Johnny will ever be a silversmith again, but he will be able to fire a gun. Johnny takes a walk while Warren prepares his surgical instruments. Looking across the landscape, at the people readying themselves for more fighting, he is filled with an intense love for his country.

ANALYSIS: CHAPTERS XI–XII
The final split between Cilla and Isannah is parallel to the final irreparable divide between the colonies and Britain. Throughout most of the turmoil leading up to the first exchange of shots, the majority of colonists still considered themselves Englishmen. After the first exchange of gunfire, however, many of these colonists no longer claimed any kinship with Britain. The split was final and radical, like the split between Cilla and Isannah, the two sisters who were once inseparable. Both splits in kinship occur in the immediate aftermath of the first battle of the war. While the colonists decide to sever their ties with Britain, Isannah does the reverse, and decides to stop identifying with her colonial family by leaving for Britain.

Lavinia Lyte weakens the strong bond between the Lapham sisters by spoiling Isannah with luxury and treating Cilla like a common servant, creating an artificial distinction of class and privilege between Cilla and Isannah. The triangle of affection between Lavinia, Isannah, and Cilla is a metaphor for the complex relationship between England, the Tories, and the Whigs. Lavinia serves as a symbol of Britain, with her wealth, her good breeding, her class-consciousness, and her love of London. We can view Isannah as a symbol for the Tories, who are loyal to Britain, many of whom rose quickly from poverty to wealth as merchants just as Isannah rose quickly from poverty to wealth when Isannah adopted her. England appealed to Tory sympathy by appealing to their desire to continue the luxurious, comfortable life they enjoyed. Similarly, Lavinia ultimately convinces Isannah to move to London by reminding her that staying in the colonies means losing her life of wealth and prestige. Isannah, in turn, behaves toward Cilla as many of the wealthy Tory families behaved toward their Whig neighbors. Forced to choose between the colonies and a future of continued privilege and luxury, the Tories chose the latter and left their old world behind.

Johnny has changed so radically during the course of the book that Lavinia's confession about his true ancestry is hardly momentous. He does not care whether the Lytes acknowledge him as kin and does not reflect on the possibility of getting a share of Lyte land. If Lavinia's confession had come earlier in the story, it would have marked a radical turning point as Johnny's great triumph of wealth. Now this admission is no longer consequential to the primary trajectory of the story. The focus of the novel is not on Johnny's personal fortune, but on his participation in the larger goal of the war effort. Similarly, Johnny no longer focuses on gaining wealth and revenge. Instead, he redirects his pride toward his country and his fellow man.

Just as Johnny has escaped from the emotional handicaps of insecurity, arrogance, and resentment, he also escapes from his physical handicap. Johnny finally allows Doctor Warren to examine his injured hand and learns that the doctor can repair some of the damage. By mending his crippled hand, Johnny shows that he has symbolically overcome his emotional handicaps as well. It is significant that Johnny only allows his hand to heal after Rab is gone. Rab's death thrusts Johnny fully into his new identity. He faces the stark reality of his terrible personal loss without self-pity and anger. Johnny's thoughts are selfless, and he focuses on the greater good of the war. He is so focused on the big picture that he is unable to feel the grief that he knows is festering inside of him.

Important Quotations Explained

1. "It is all another way of saying—God's way of
    saying—that pride goeth before a fall."

Johnny speaks these words in the first chapter to reiterate the lesson
that Mr. Lapham has just tried to teach him about the sin of pride.
Johnny can paraphrase the words of the Bible, but he is not yet pre-
pared to truly believe the words in his heart. At this point in the
novel, Johnny's arrogance and pride guide his behavior toward others. He constantly bullies the two other apprentices in the Lapham
household, and he is unable to empathize with others. Johnny is
unwilling to struggle against his pride and instead prefers to indulge
it. This quote describes the notion of pride preceding a fall, which
foreshadows Johnny's coming accident, an accident that is the direct
result of his pride. Ironically, if Johnny had responded positively to
Mr. Lapham's lesson rather than ignoring it entirely, he might have
developed into an arrogant, proud man. If Johnny had listened to
Mr. Lapham and tried to rein in his pride, then Dove would not have
played his practical joke, and Johnny's hand would not have been
injured. It is Johnny's injury, however, that forces him to examine
himself and struggle toward a new, less arrogant identity. Without
this traumatic accident, Johnny might not have met Rab and the
Lornes or become involved in the Whig rebellion. Therefore, he
might never have developed into an empathetic, patient, self-assured
young man.

2. "Don't touch me! Don't touch me with that dreadful hand!"

Isannah Lapham speaks these words in Chapter III, driving Johnny to the lowest point of his despair. Because of his handicap, Johnny is now unemployed and broke. Once Isannah expresses her disgust toward his disfigurement, Johnny also feels that he does not have any friends or loved ones. Isannah's statement is a catalyst for a series of events that affect the rest of Johnny's life. Because of her words, Johnny feels he has no other recourse than to approach Lyte with the silver cup, which leads to his arrest and his relationship with Rab and the Lornes. Isannah's exclamation also reveals her true character. Johnny has just given Isannah a gift, then tried to hug and kiss her, when she makes this outburst. Her response to Johnny's affection and kindness reveals Isannah's selfishness and lack of sensitivity toward others and her inability to consider anyone's feelings but her own. These words foreshadow Isannah's choice of a life of luxury over a life with her loved ones, when she decides to join the Lytes and move to London.

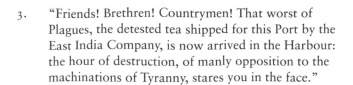

3. "Friends! Brethren! Countrymen! That worst of Plagues, the detested tea shipped for this Port by the East India Company, is now arrived in the Harbour: the hour of destruction, of manly opposition to the machinations of Tyranny, stares you in the face."

This quote appears in Chapter VI, as part of Samuel Adams's rally cry. Adams writes this passage to rouse up the colonists against the shipment of tea that the British are forcing the Bostonians to purchase. Adams and the other rebel leaders view the shipment as an act of British tyranny and another instance of "taxation without representation," since the colonists must pay a small tax on the tea. When the British governor of Boston refuses to send the pricey tea back to England, the rebellious Whigs organize a controlled act of violence, now known as the Boston Tea Party. Young men, dressed as Native Americans, board the ship and throw all of the tea overboard. Historically, this act of rebellion was the most dramatic one the colonists had ever staged, and it drew a strong punishment from the British government: the port of Boston was closed. The Boston Tea Party was significant because it set off a series of events that led to the Revolutionary War. The colonists were outraged by Britain's stiff penalties, such as the Intolerable Acts and the closing of Boston's harbor. As a result, the colonists banded together to fight against the injustice and declared a war for independence. Adams's quote expresses the anger and frustration of the colonists that caused them to unite against the British and emerge as a new, independent country.

Adams's quote is also important because it shows how the Whigs tried to unify the colonists against the British by making them seem like an inhuman enemy. Many colonists still had ties to the British and considered themselves English citizens. Adams realizes that it is difficult to fight against a country if you feel you are fighting against your family members, lovers, or friends. Adams chooses his language carefully, and forces a distinction between the colonists ("us") and the British ("them"). He speaks to the colonists, whom he calls friends, family, and countrymen, and the "manly opposition," showing that the colonists are human beings, fighting for human rights. He asks the colonists to fight against the British, whom he describes as an inhuman face and an unnatural machine—a technological monster clamping down on the rights of humanity.

4. "There shall be no more tyranny. A handful of men cannot seize power over thousands. A man shall choose who it is shall rule over him. . . . We give all we have, lives, property, safety, skills . . . we fight, we die, for a simple thing. Only that a man can stand up."

James Otis speaks these words in Chapter VIII. Otis is brilliant but insane, so he has not been involved in the Boston Observers even though he was a founder. Nonetheless, Otis speaks these words as part of a rousing speech at one of the Boston Observers' meetings. Here Otis offers his idealistic vision of what the American Revolution seeks to achieve: an independent nation based on the principles of freedom and equality, where the rights of every man are the same, regardless of class, wealth, and religion. His lofty sentiments inspire everyone in the room, particularly Johnny, and he helps to unite the audience against the British government. "So that a man can stand up" becomes Johnny's personal war cry, and he repeats it to himself in moments of doubt. Johnny does not admire Otis's sentiments merely because Otis is an articulate, enthusiastic speaker. Rather, Johnny rationally believes that human beings each have the natural right to liberty and freedom.

5.   The cow that lowed, the man who milked, the chickens
      that came running and the woman who called them,
      the fragrance streaming from the plowed land and the
      plowman. These he possessed. . . . The wood smoke
      rising from the home-hearths rose from his heart.

This passage from Chapter XII describes how Johnny develops his
sense of self and his sense of country simultaneously. In the aftermath of the first battle of the Revolutionary War, Johnny looks
around at his countrymen, who are optimistically preparing themselves for war. He finally realizes who he is and what identity he has
been seeking—he is an American. He is a patriot, a soldier, an idealistic believer, and he believes in the equal rights of man. Until this
moment, Johnny has modeled himself on Rab and has tried to com-
port himself based on Rab's beliefs and behavior. But now Rab is
dead, and Johnny realizes that he is an independent person and more
than just Rab's follower. He has developed into someone who feels
strongly about a cause. Without Rab, he must now govern his own
actions based on his own ideology. Likewise, Johnny realizes how
important it is for America to fight for its own right to govern itself,
and he is ready to fight for this goal.

QUOTATIONS

KEY FACTS

FULL TITLE
  Johnny Tremain

AUTHOR
  Esther Forbes

TYPE OF WORK
  Novel

GENRE
  Coming-of-age story; historical fiction; war fiction

LANGUAGE
  English

TIME AND PLACE WRITTEN
  Esther Forbes began to write *Johnny Tremain* on December 8,
  1941, the day after Pearl Harbor was bombed. She worked on
  the novel at her home in Massachusetts, completing it in 1943.

DATE OF FIRST PUBLICATION
  1943

PUBLISHER
  Houghton Mifflin

NARRATOR
  The novel is narrated by an anonymous voice.

POINT OF VIEW
  The narrator speaks in the third person, focusing on Johnny's
  actions and experiences. The narrator primarily describes events
  subjectively, as Johnny experiences them, but occasionally
  reveals pieces of information that Johnny does not know.

TONE
  The narrator does not participate in the story, but shows
  sympathy and hope for nearly all the characters in the novel.

TENSE
  Present

SETTING (TIME)
The book takes place during the years immediately preceding the Revolutionary War. The story begins in the summer of 1773 and ends during April of 1775.

SETTING (PLACE)
Colonial Boston

PROTAGONIST
Johnny Tremain

MAJOR CONFLICT
Johnny struggles to overcome his arrogance and selfishness and to develop into an independent, humble, generous, and patient young man. Similarly, the colonists struggle to gain independence from the oppressive British government.

RISING ACTION
Johnny's hand is disfigured and disabled because of Dove's careless prank; Johnny must find a new trade; Johnny meets Rab, moves into the Lorne house, and delivers newspapers; Johnny befriends Whig leaders and becomes a spy for the rebellion; Johnny participates in the Boston Tea Party; the British soldiers descend on Lexington.

CLIMAX
The war begins between the colonists and the British; Johnny learns of Rab's death during the battle of Lexington and completes his break from his past arrogant self.

FALLING ACTION
Doctor Warren tells Johnny that he can fix his disfigured hand; Johnny is proud of his country.

THEMES
War's transformation of boys into men; revolution as a coming-of-age; the influence of personal relationships on character

MOTIFS
Pride; forgiveness; class

SYMBOLS
Johnny's crippled hand; the silver Lyte cup; Johnny's infatuation with Lavinia Lyte

FORESHADOWING

Mr. Lapham's repeated warnings that "pride goeth before a fall," which foreshadows Johnny's accident; Johnny's struggles with Lyte and Stranger foreshadows the unequal struggle between the colonies and Britain; Johnny's obsession with the eyes of muskets foreshadows Rab's death

KEY FACTS

STUDY QUESTIONS & ESSAY TOPICS

STUDY QUESTIONS

1. *In what ways is Johnny Tremain's life shaped by the social and economic practices of colonial America on the eve of the Revolution? What does the novel reveal about these practices?*

In the time period leading up to the Revolutionary War, the customs and values of the colonies were evolving. Some traditional practices were still in place, while others were slowly changing. Although America had begun separating from England, the colonies still followed some of its traditional socioeconomic practices. For example, in colonial Boston, education was not compulsory. Although literacy was higher in the colonies than in England, the ability to read, write, and do simple arithmetic was considered a solid education outside the upper class. Unless a child came from a wealthy family, his or her labor was necessary to his or her family's support. Families paid skilled artisans to take their sons in as apprentices. In return for the valuable training the apprentice received, all products of the apprentice's labor belonged to his master for seven years. As a result, Johnny begins training and working as a silversmith from a very young age. Because his parents are deceased, he is fortunate to live with the Laphams, who are a middle-class family. Johnny had an incredible opportunity for upward mobility by working with a skilled tradesman like Mr. Lapham. Thus, his dream of owning a silver shop in colonial America is realistic. Johnny would not have this opportunity if he lived in England, where social class dictated one's station in life.

2.   *What does* Johnny Tremain *reveal about marriage customs in colonial America?*

While it is true that colonial Americans enjoyed more social mobility than the inhabitants of Britain, the marriage possibilities available to colonials were still determined to a large extent by their social class. Mrs. Lapham is eager to marry one of her daughters to Johnny because there are no sons to inherit the silver shop. Moreover, Johnny is her father-in-law's most promising apprentice, and, there-fore, the one with the most future earning potential. Although he is only fourteen years old, Johnny is a good marriage prospect for any middle-class family in colonial America. Social status, and not love, often influenced relationships in America, just like in England. How-ever, although it was normal to marry for money and not love, many younger colonials did marry for love, suggesting a separation from British customs. For example, Dorcas will not marry Mr. Tweedie to keep the silver shop in the Lapham family; instead she marries the poverty-stricken Frizel, Jr., because she falls in love with him.

3.   *What role does religion play in Johnny Tremain's world?*

Religion plays an important role in Johnny's colonial world because it directly affects laws and societal norms. A person could be punished for not observing religious law, such as the decree against working on Sundays. However, at the time in which the novel is set, some religious restrictions on colonial society were becoming more relaxed. Mr. Lapham is strictly pious, but his family regards him as old-fashioned. Mrs. Lapham encourages Johnny to finish John Hancock's basin on time by working on Sunday, for example. The younger generation embraced more relaxed religious attitudes, partly because of the increasingly cosmopolitan character of the city, and also because of an ideological shift from religion to science as a source of truth and enlightenment. As a result, Johnny and other colonials routinely break old religious practices. Thus, the Boston Observers can meet on Sunday and secretly plan their rebellion against England.

4. *Contrast James Otis's rousing speech about the need for revolution with Samuel Adams's attitude toward rebellion. Which do you think Johnny finds more appealing, and why?*

The novel suggests that Samuel Adams and James Otis had very different attitudes toward the revolution. Adams's personal history implies that he may want to start a war with Britain out of revenge. The British Parliament ruined his father's finances by destroying the bank where he kept his money. Adams's rhetoric expresses his anger and outrage at the British, as evidenced by his posters and propaganda. He tries to rouse the colonists to resist British rule by using words that convey that England is an inhuman, machine-like enemy. He does not focus on the natural rights of man and the independent spirit of the colonists. Rather, Adams expresses how the British government is oppressive, a tyranny that is destroying the lives of the colonists. War is a necessary evil that the colonists must use to gain their independence from such a tyrannical government.

On the other hand, James Otis wants to fight so that "a man can stand up." He challenges Adams's reasons for fighting the war, which are not for peace but for destruction and conflict. Otis wants the colonists to have the right to choose who rules over them, and not fight simply to protect the money of the Americans. His rousing speech to the Boston Observers focuses on the natural rights that free men should enjoy. He has an idealistic vision of an independent America; however, he cannot drive the colonists to war merely on ideals and hopes. Adams's passion and fervor, coupled with Otis's reasons and ideals, ignite the revolutionary spirit.

James Otis may have loftier reasons than Samuels Adams for inspiring the Revolutionary War. However, the end result is the same, which is that many colonists will sacrifice their lives, and kill many innocent British men, to achieve American independence. Samuel Adams did his duty, and he was able to incite many colonists to fight the war, particularly when many Americans were still loyal to the British. However, Otis provided the colonists with rational, heartfelt reasons for fighting the war. At first, Johnny is similar to Adams, and he searches for ways to get revenge instead of to forgive. Later, Johnny redirects his passions and fervor and wants to fight for the rights of his fellow men. Thus, Johnny's patriotism toward his country is based on both Otis's and Adams's attitudes. Otis's soft, low voice and Adams's passion are appealing in different ways.

When Johnny dreams about the lobsters with human eyes, he also sees how both sides of the war effort are unappealing: Hancock's pity of humanity and Adams's pleasure at cruelty. Ironically, both of these attitudes led to a war that caused the loss of human lives, and also the freedom of the human spirit.

QUESTIONS & ESSAYS

SUGGESTED ESSAY TOPICS

1.   How does Jonathan Lyte serve as a foil to Johnny? How does their relationship dramatize the tension between the colonies and Britain?

2.   Compare how Rab and the Lornes influence Johnny's psychological development.

3.   How does *Johnny Tremain* address race in colonial America?

4.   Why is the relationship between the colonists and British troops complex and often ambivalent?

5.   Do you think Johnny Tremain would have helped the Whigs in their fight for independence if he had not injured his hand?

REVIEW & RESOURCES

QUIZ

1. Which of the following trades does Johnny wish to pursue at the beginning of the novel?

    A. Accounting
    B. Blacksmithing
    C. Silversmithing
    D. Printing

2. Why does Johnny bully Dove?

    A. Dove is lazy.
    B. Johnny is arrogant.
    C. Johnny is proud.
    D. All of the above

3. Why does Mr. Lapham disapprove of Johnny's arrogance?

    A. Johnny does not have the talent to justify his pride.
    B. Mr. Lapham is a devout Christian who believes men should be humble.
    C. Mr. Lapham is jealous of Johnny's talent.
    D. Mr. Lapham harbors an irrational dislike of Johnny.

4. Why does Hancock commission Mr. Lapham to make a sugar basin for a tea set?

    A. Mr. Lapham was the original craftsman of the set.
    B. Mr. Lapham has a reputation for making beautiful, elaborate tea sets.
    C. Hancock has heard of Johnny's great talent, so he wants to see it in action.
    D. Hancock confuses Mr. Lapham with Paul Revere.

5. Why doesn't Johnny accept Paul Revere's offer to buy the remaining time on his contract with Mr. Lapham?

   A. Paul Revere is not as good at silversmithing as Mr. Lapham.
   B. Johnny is in love with Cilla and does not want to leave her.
   C. Johnny is the chief breadwinner in the Lapham household.
   D. Johnny is too busy training to be a Minute Man.

6. How does Johnny injure his hand?

   A. Dove deliberately hands him a cracked crucible that bursts when Johnny uses it.
   B. Johnny accidentally picks up a hot piece of metal.
   C. Dove pushes him onto the stove while he is working.
   D. Dove pours molten silver over his hand.

7. Johnny is related to which of the following wealthy Boston merchants?

   A. John Hancock
   B. Paul Revere
   C. Jonathan Lyte
   D. Samuel Adams

8. What does Rab think about Jonathan Lyte?

   A. Rab thinks Lyte is an honest, upstanding citizen.
   B. Rab thinks Lyte is crooked because he plays both the Tory and Whig sides for profit.
   C. Rab respects Lyte for being consistent and honest in his political views, even though Lyte is a Tory.
   D. Rab pretends to like Lyte because he has a crush on his daughter, Lavinia.

9. How does Jonathan Lyte react when Johnny presents the silver cup as proof of their kinship?

   A. He accuses Johnny of stealing the cup and has him arrested.
   B. He welcomes Johnny into the family with open arms.
   C. He is not happy, but he wants to do the right thing by giving Johnny his share of the Lyte fortune.
   D. He throws Johnny out of his house because he thinks Johnny is a liar.

10. Who comes to Johnny's aid after he is arrested on charges of stealing a silver cup from Jonathan Lyte?

    A. John Hancock
    B. Rab Silsbee
    C. Dove
    D. Mr. Lapham

11. Whose testimony clears Johnny at his trial?

    A. Josiah Quincy's
    B. Mrs. Lapham's
    C. Dove's
    D. Cilla Lapham's

12. What job does Dove take after Mr. Lapham fires him?

    A. He becomes Lieutenant Stranger's stable boy.
    B. He becomes a clerk for Jonathan Lyte.
    C. He becomes Colonel Smith's stable boy.
    D. He becomes Paul Revere's apprentice.

13. Why does Lavinia Lyte take Isannah to live with her?

    A. Isannah's ethereal beauty enchants her.
    B. She needs a personal servant.
    C. Mrs. Lapham cannot afford to support Isannah any longer.
    D. Lavinia wants to live with Cilla, who will not consent to do so unless Isannah comes too.

14. How does Lavinia weaken the bond between Isannah and Cilla?

    A. She tells Isannah that Cilla does not love her anymore.
    B. She treats Cilla like a common servant and Isannah like a prized pet.
    C. She refuses to allow Isannah to see Cilla.
    D. She confesses her own love for Johnny.

15. Why do the Observers begin leaving James Otis out of their meetings?

    A. They suspect that Otis is a Tory spy.
    B. They believe that Otis is mentally unstable.
    C. They fear that Otis does not take the need for secrecy seriously enough.
    D. They do not think Otis is articulate or intelligent.

16. Why do Johnny and Rab toss Dove overboard during the Boston Tea Party?

    A. Johnny catches Dove stealing tea, a violation of the ethics of political protest.
    B. They want to get revenge against Dove for his role in the accident that disfigured Johnny's hand.
    C. They take pleasure in bullying Dove.
    D. They think Dove is a British spy.

17. How does England react to the Boston Tea Party?

    A. England agrees to let the colonies have political representation.
    B. England refuses to give the colonies political representation, but they revoke all taxes on imported goods.
    C. England hangs some of the culprits.
    D. England closes the port of Boston in an attempt to force the city to pay for the tea.

REVIEW & RESOURCES

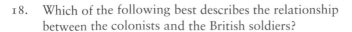

18. Which of the following best describes the relationship between the colonists and the British soldiers?

    A.   The relationship is completely acrimonious.

    B.   The relationship is often tense, but many soldiers and colonists have no particular animosity toward one another.

    C.   The relationship is not acrimonious at all.

    D.   The relationship is characterized by whining and petty bickering punctuated by brief displays of affection and exchanges of gifts.

19. Why does Pumpkin want to desert the British army?

    A.   He wants to own his own farm, which is easy to achieve in the colonies and very difficult in England.

    B.   He is often mistreated by his commanding officer.

    C.   He is in love with an American girl.

    D.   He does not want to fight against the colonies.

20. Which of the following best describes Johnny's relationship with Lieutenant Stranger?

    A.   It is an amicable relationship between equals.

    B.   Although it is an amicable relationship, Lieutenant Stranger always treats Johnny as his social inferior.

    C.   It is a relationship full of bitter animosity.

    D.   Where horsemanship is concerned, Lieutenant Stranger treats Johnny like an equal, but in all other situations he treats Johnny as his inferior.

21. Why did Johnny's father use an assumed name in Boston?

    A.   He was evading arrest.

    B.   He was impersonating a French nobleman.

    C.   He was ashamed to be a prisoner of war.

    D.   He was an American spy.

REVIEW & RESOURCES

22. What happens to Rab in the battle at Lexington?

    A. The British capture him.

    B. He is mortally wounded.

    C. He survives the battle and escapes to the Lorne house.

    D. He receives a light wound.

23. When does the reality of armed conflict hit Johnny?

    A. When he witnesses Pumpkin's execution

    B. When he first learns that Rab is mortally wounded

    C. When he sees injured British soldiers returning to Boston

    D. When he hears the names of the first colonists to die in armed conflict with British soldiers

24. Why does it take so long for the Lytes to acknowledge Johnny as kin?

    A. The family of Johnny's father did not tell them that Johnny's mother had a child.

    B. Johnny's father used an assumed name in Boston.

    C. The family of Johnny's mother disowned her for marrying Johnny's father.

    D. All of the above

25. Who eventually repairs Johnny's injured hand?

    A. A British surgeon

    B. Doctor Church

    C. Johnny's hand is never fixed

    D. Doctor Warren

ANSWER KEY:

1: C; 2: D; 3: B; 4: A; 5: C; 6: A; 7: C; 8: B; 9: A; 10: B; 11: D; 12: C; 13: A; 14: B; 15: B; 16: A; 17: D; 18: B; 19: A; 20: D; 21: C; 22: B; 23: A; 24: D; 25: D

SUGGESTIONS FOR FURTHER READING

ELLIS, JOSEPH J. *Founding Brothers: The Revolutionary Generation.* New York: Alfred A. Knopf, 2000.

FERLINS, JOHN E. *Setting the World Ablaze: Washington, Adams, Jefferson, and the American Revolution.* New York: Oxford University Press, 2000.

FORBES, ESTHER. *America's Paul Revere.* New York: Houghton Mifflin, 1976.

———. *Paul Revere: The World He Lived In.* New York: Houghton Mifflin, 1999.

HAKIM, JOY. *From Colonies to Country.* Oxford: Oxford University Press, 1999.

HALLAN, WILLIAM H. *The Day the American Revolution Began: Nineteen April 1775.* New York: Harper Perennial Library, 2001.

"Meet Esther Forbes." Glencoe Literary Library. www.glencoe.com.

REVIEW & RESOURCES

A Note on the Type

The typeface used in SparkNotes study guides is Sabon, created by master typographer Jan Tschichold in 1964. Tschichold revolutionized the field of graphic design twice: first with his use of asymmetrical layouts and sanserif type in the 1930s when he was affiliated with the Bauhaus, then by abandoning assymetry and calling for a return to the classic ideals of design. Sabon, his only extant typeface, is emblematic of his latter program: Tschichold's design is a recreation of the types made by Claude Garamond, the great French typographer of the Renaissance, and his contemporary Robert Granjon. Fittingly, it is named for Garamond's apprentice, Jacques Sabon.

SPARKNOTES
TEST PREPARATION
GUIDES

The SparkNotes team figured it was time to cut standardized tests down to size. We've studied the tests for you, so that SparkNotes test prep guides are:

Smarter:
Packed with critical-thinking skills and test-
taking strategies that will improve your score.

Better:
Fully up to date, covering all new features of the tests,
with study tips on every type of question.

Faster:
Our books cover exactly what you need to
know for the test. No more, no less.

SparkNotes Guide to the SAT & PSAT
SparkNotes Guide to the SAT & PSAT — Deluxe Internet Edition
SparkNotes Guide to the ACT
SparkNotes Guide to the ACT — Deluxe Internet Edition
SparkNotes Guide to the SAT II Writing
SparkNotes Guide to the SAT II U.S. History
SparkNotes Guide to the SAT II Math Ic
SparkNotes Guide to the SAT II Math IIc
SparkNotes Guide to the SAT II Biology
SparkNotes Guide to the SAT II Physics

SPARKNOTES STUDY GUIDES: